SIX STEPS TO AN EMOTIONALLY INTELLIGENT TEENAGER

Teaching Social Skills to Your Teen

James Windell

John Wiley & Sons, Inc.

New York • Chichester • Weinheim • Brisbane • Singapore • Toronto

This book is printed on acid-free paper. ∞

Copyright © 1999 by James Windell. All rights reserved

Published by John Wiley & Sons, Inc.
Published simultaneously in Canada

No part of this publication may be reproduced, stored in a retrieval system or transmitted in any form or by any means, electronic, mechanical, photocopying, recording, scanning or otherwise, except as permitted under Sections 107 or 108 of the 1976 United States Copyright Act, without either the prior written permission of the Publisher, or authorization through payment of the appropriate per-copy fee to the Copyright Clearance Center, 222 Rosewood Drive, Danvers, MA 01923, (978) 750-8400, fax (978) 750-4744. Requests to the Publisher for permission should be addressed to the Permissions Department, John Wiley & Sons, Inc., 605 Third Avenue, New York, NY 10158-0012, (212) 850-6011, fax (212) 850-6008, E-Mail: PERMREQ @ WILEY.COM.

This publication is designed to provide accurate and authoritative information in regard to the subject matter covered. It is sold with the understanding that the publisher is not engaged in rendering professional services. If professional advice or other expert assistance is required, the services of a competent professional person should be sought.

Library of Congress Cataloging-in-Publication Data:

Windell, James.
    Six steps to an emotionally intelligent teenager : teaching social
    skills to your teen / James Windell.
       p.   cm.
    Includes index.
    ISBN 0-471-29767-4 (pbk. : alk. paper)
    1. Parent and teenager. 2. Social skills. 3. Problem children—
  Behavior modification. 4. Adolescent psychology. I. Title.
  II. Title: 6 steps to an emotionally intelligent teenager.
  HQ799.15.W58   1999
  649'.125—dc21   99-11239

Printed in the United States of America

10 9 8 7 6 5 4 3 2 1

CONTENTS

7 STEP SIX: TEACH YOUR TEENAGER TO RESOLVE CONFLICTS PEACEFULLY

PART THREE

PARENTING THE DIFFICULT TEEN

ACKNOWLEDGMENTS

I would like to thank several people who contributed to this book. First, I'd like to acknowledge and thank Bernard Gaulier, the chief of the Psychological Clinic at the Oakland County Probate Court and Family Division. His support and encouragement have allowed me to pursue my ideas in developing the adolescent group therapy program there.

My colleagues in that clinic, chiefly Vickie Rupert, Rod Yeacker, and Karen Wiater, were especially helpful in reading drafts of this book and giving me valuable feedback. Their willingness to make suggestions and provide honest criticism are appreciated. Karen deserves special kudos for providing me with anecdotes which have enriched this book.

My thanks to my wife, Ellen, and my children, Jason and Jill, for allowing me to use details of our family life to illustrate several points throughout this book.

I am especially appreciative of Judith McCarthy, the editor who believed in this book and gave me such important help throughout this project.

My agent, Denise Marcil, has been a loyal supporter of my books, even when the initial ideas lacked merit or were not fully developed. She has never failed to help me formulate my ideas and then to find publishers for my books. For that I will always be grateful.

Finally, this book would not have been possible without the hundreds of adolescents whom I've seen in individual and group psychotherapy over the course of my career. Each of them has contributed something valuable to my education. Most of them are in their own way responsible for this book by constantly reminding me of their resiliency, challenging me with their uniqueness, and convincing me of their ability to make positive changes.

INTRODUCTION

I n 1991, I was a happy psychologist teaching parents of delinquents how to be better parents. A few years before that, I had been hired at the Oakland County Juvenile Court in metropolitan Detroit to develop a parent training program. Creating that new program was a satisfying experience, and it allowed me to develop my own ideas about how to parent difficult adolescents. With my role as a teacher came the enjoyment of helping parents improve their skills. However, the chief of the Psychological Clinic of the Juvenile Court came to me one day and offered me the chance to take over a new job: running treatment groups with adolescent delinquents.

I did not jump at the chance, and I spent several days thinking about it and what I would be giving up. As I discussed this offer with my wife, Ellen, we both were aware that shifting from a job I thoroughly enjoyed to one that had trouble written all over it would not be easy to do. Ellen advised me to turn it down.

I felt comfortable and safe teaching parents. Why, at this time in my career, should I give that up and instead deal with defiant, resistant, and oppositional kids? I couldn't think of a good reason at the time. But a voice deep down inside told me that if I was this comfortable with parents and if I feared going into the trenches with troubled teenagers, then I really ought to do it. So I did.

Later, one of my rationalizations for such an irrational decision had to do with my comfort with teaching parents to use better discipline skills. Because my own children were already adults, I wondered at times if I was giving parents the best possible advice about disciplining tough teens. I needed to confirm for myself that the discipline methods I advised parents to use with difficult kids really would work.

The result has been an exhilarating, challenging experience

1

that has taught me a great deal about the difficulties and the satisfactions of working with delinquent adolescents. Some of what I've learned from working with oppositional children I wrote about in my book *Children Who Say No When You Want Them to Say Yes*. *Six Steps* is a continuation of my efforts to communicate to parents what I've learned about dealing with tough kids.

I knew before taking on the group treatment assignment that traditional group therapy techniques do not bring about changes in delinquents. Tough teens do not respond well to sitting around talking about feelings and to efforts to try to help them develop insight. The research at the time indicated that a social skills approach would help many difficult teenagers to learn to deal better with their anger, their impulsivity, and their tendency to resolve conflicts in violent ways.

It is clear that too many teenagers in the 1990s, both in and out of the judicial system, lack the social skills to handle their feelings and their interactions with others in peaceful, appropriate ways. When I became adept at teaching social skills to the teenagers in my groups, I wanted to pass on this knowledge to parents—the people who need specialized help the most. This book is an explanation of how you can teach your teen the social skills he or she needs to be a kid you can be proud of.

Let's use two kids, Nick Collins and Kelly Kulich, as examples. Throughout this book I've used real stories but have changed all names for privacy.

Nick Collins gets bored easily at school. A 13-year-old who has always had difficulty concentrating and dealing with his restlessness, Nick also has trouble handling his anger. His mother, a single parent, says Nick is basically a good boy. "However," Dorothy Collins says, "Nick has got to learn not to get so angry. That's his biggest problem. Nick gets mad at a teacher, and he gets up and walks out of his class. Then he gets sent to the office or suspended, and then the school is calling me. I try to punish him, but what am I supposed to do?"

If Nick's mother sees his difficulties as a discipline or behavior problem, she will continue to try punishment or other corrective action to bring about a change in his behavior. By turning to a traditional notion of discipline to handle Nick's problems, she runs the risk of never focusing on the real difficulty Nick has, and he may continue to have social problems much of his life.

"My daughter Kelly has been headstrong since the day she was born," reports Debra Kulich, the mother of 16-year-old Kelly. "If she wants to do something, she keeps asking and pleading to do it until I give in. I know I shouldn't give in, but I can't handle her anger and the temper tantrums she throws. It's just not worth it."

At school, Kelly gets mad easily with other kids. When she's mad, she flies into rages at which time she often physically attacks the other person. She swears, scratches, bites, or pushes anyone who crosses her at these times. Debra has always had concerns about Kelly's anger. Maybe, she has thought, she should have punished Kelly more in order to have taught her to control herself better.

Like Dorothy Collins, Debra can either view Kelly's behavior as requiring corrective discipline, or she can see it as a special opportunity to teach Kelly. If Debra reframes Kelly's anger and frustration as golden opportunities to teach her better anger control, she can help Kelly learn important social skills that will last a lifetime.

Over the past several years as I have worked with more difficult children and teens along with their parents, I have come to realize that parents rely too much on punishment and too little on teaching kids what they need to know. Most difficult and troubled teens—the ones who fight, steal, get in trouble with the police, are truant from school, and have little regard for the rights of others—

are kids who typically lack social skills. Even though it may appear at first glance that the problems of Kelly and Nick are not at all similar, they are. It is true that Kelly's problems involve fights with peers and her mother, whereas Nick's trouble occurs mostly at school. It is also true that Nick's problems involve poor relations with teachers and that Kelly's problems have as much to do with poor impulse control as with difficulty calming herself when frustrated or angry. Yet because both of these teenager's problems involve relationships with other people, they are called *social skills problems* or *social skills deficits*. When children and teens fail to develop good social skills, they are likely to be unhappy because they experience rejection, are alienated from peers and potential friends, and lack the ability to manage emotions or to adroitly handle interpersonal conflict.

Social skills are the ability to be competent in dealing with others. Social competence involves judgment in interpersonal relations, emotional control, and an understanding of what is appropriate social behavior.

Many of the teenagers I work with in group treatment *know* what is right and appropriate social behavior, but they are either unable or unwilling to act on that knowledge. Some, of course, are seemingly clueless about how they present themselves to people or how others react to them. When a child has the ability to see himself the way others see him, he can adjust his behavior so he is more accepted and a better friend. In addition, this kind of child can learn from his social mistakes so that his relationships with other people remain rather stable or even improve.

Many kids are born with temperaments that predispose them to more difficulty becoming socially skilled. For these children, especially, it is extremely important that they learn social skills as early as possible.

Research shows that social adjustment is an important part of growing up. When children are not popular or accepted by their peers, they tend to struggle in many areas of their lives. Studies clearly demonstrate that children who are not accepted by others not only have more interpersonal problems than their more popular or better accepted peers but also have more learning and achievement problems.

It is never too late for adolescents to learn to be socially adept. But it takes patience and some specialized knowledge to teach them the social skills they need to be more successful. My experience with hundreds of adolescents tells me that although social skills problems often start early in life and typically lead to chronic difficulties in getting along with others, they are not unchangeable. The problem is that less than half of the teens with social skills problems are identified and helped at an early age.

When you understand that your teen has a social skills problem, you are in a much better position to help her make important changes in her life. You have the power to do this because other studies show that teenagers are not at the end of development. They can still learn and develop social skills. Most adolescents are still trying to establish a unique identity. And while they are trying to figure out who they are, teens can readily learn new social skills and put them to practical use.

The social skills training you can provide, which will emphasize self-expression in socially acceptable ways, leads to important benefits for your teenager. Among those benefits are an enhanced self-concept, better self-esteem, an improved ability to control his own destiny, and the ability to resist negative influences.

Because teens can't understand and empathize with others, close and intimate relationships are fraught with difficulty and misunderstanding.

Because they can't handle anger well, they blow up easily, get angry often, and let a bad temper or angry outbursts control their lives, their jobs, and their relationships.

Because they are frequently aggressive and often cannot resolve conflicts in peaceful ways, they drive others away and have no ready resources for settling conflicts and disputes. Not only do these circumstances cause heartache, they also lead to frequent changes in relationships, jobs, or in extreme cases brushes with the law.

A socially intelligent adolescent is one who can get along with others, has the ability to monitor his or her own behavior, is able to stay calm when upset or angry, and knows how to successfully solve conflicts. Wouldn't you like your child to fit that description? He or she can.

Your family serves as the important training center for your teen to learn social and emotional intelligence. You shape the behavior of your teen. It is in your home that your child is trained to respond to others, to manage anger, to control impulsivity, and to deal with authority.

My work with many families has confirmed that how everyone in your family gets along with one another and how you give rewards and praise help to determine whether your teenager will be successful in interpersonal skills. Also, it is within your family that your adolescent will learn the skills that teach him to keep anger under control and to solve problems in appropriate ways.

Specifically, the most important factors in how your teen develops emotional intelligence have to do with how you handle guidance and discipline. Your teen will develop good social skills if you are consistent in your handling of discipline, if you avoid using harsh punishment, if you set limits, if you reward acceptable behaviors, if you seldom use threats, and if you rarely give in to stubborn behavior.

When you handle discipline and guidance in this way, there is a greater opportunity for your teen to become adept at solving problems without resorting to anger and aggression in her personal relationships. How you use the suggestions and activities I recommend could spell the difference between success and failure in your child's life as well as between harmony and chaos in your home.

It helps to begin early in life, but this doesn't mean that you can't teach social skills to your child at later ages. Most people can learn to improve their social skills throughout childhood and adolescence, so don't give up on your child. You can take advantage of what I call "golden opportunities" to make a serious impact on your child at any age.

Chapter 1 will first help you determine whether you need to be concerned about your teen and then tell you what you need to know in order to be a skilled teacher of emotional intelligence to your adolescent. Chapters 2 through 8 will give you the tools to teach your adolescent to be more highly skilled in interpersonal relationships.

I am convinced, based on my work with families and with difficult teenagers, that knowing how and when to teach social skills makes all the difference. But part of your ability to be an effective teacher will depend on your attitude and your willingness to recognize and capitalize on the opportunities available to you.

As you read on, you will discover how to look for and even create these opportunities, how to understand and model social skills in your own life to benefit your children, and how to best teach the skills your adolescent will need in order to be successful in life.

PART ONE

PREPARING TO TEACH SOCIAL SKILLS TO YOUR TEEN

1

WHAT YOU NEED TO KNOW ABOUT TEACHING SOCIAL SKILLS

Maybe you're not sure if you need this book. I've designed a short quiz to help you decide if your teenager has a social skills problem and if you ought to be concerned. You can use this quiz to figure out how your teen is developing and on what areas he or she needs to work.

DOES YOUR TEEN NEED SOCIAL SKILLS COACHING?

	Yes	No
1. Has my teenager been suspended from school more than once?	___	___
2. Has my teenager ever been arrested and charged with a crime?	___	___
3. Has my teenager on more than one occasion broken something valuable, punched a hole in the wall, or hurt his/her fist or hand out of anger?	___	___
4. Has my teenager been involved in more than one physical fight in the past year?	___	___

	Yes	No
5. Does my teenager throw angry fits or temper tantrums until I give in?	___	___
6. Does my teenager lack goals for the future?	___	___
7. Does my teenager avoid planning his time?	___	___
8. Does my teenager consistently blame others for his/her problems?	___	___
9. Has my teenager been drunk more than once or been high on drugs more than once?	___	___
10. Does my teenager engage in the same self-defeating behaviors even though they keep him/her from achieving goals?	___	___
11. Does my teenager think others are out to get him/her?	___	___
12. Has my teenager ever been physically abusive toward a boyfriend or a girlfriend?	___	___
13. Does my teenager have difficulty identifying his/her emotions as anger, sadness, happiness, or fear?	___	___
14. Does my teenager have difficulty readily identifying other people's feelings?	___	___
15. Does my teenager have trouble talking about conflicts and problems?	___	___
16. Does my teenager frequently use aggressive methods to solve problems and conflicts?	___	___
17. Has my teenager failed to develop ways to talk about or work his/her way out of uncomfortable situations, like disappointment and frustration?	___	___
18. Is my teenager too passive?	___	___

	Yes	No
19. Does my teenager have a history of being bullied or victimized by peers?	___	___
20. Does my teenager bully or intimidate peers, friends, or even family members?	___	___

If you answer yes to two or less of these questions, the chances are that your teenager only sometimes lacks some of the important social skills and has, therefore, only mild social skills deficits. If you answer yes to as many as three but no more than five questions, your teen has moderate social skills problems. And if you answer yes to six or more, your teen has serious social skills difficulties.

To address social skills problems related to your teenager's difficulties in goal setting, refer to Chapter 2. If your teen needs help with identifying and changing self-defeating behaviors, read Chapter 3. For more information about helping your teen be more assertive, go to Chapter 4. To teach your teen to have more feelings toward others, read Chapter 5. To address the problem of anger in your teen, read Chapter 6. And if you wish to teach your teen to learn to solve problems in more peaceful ways, read Chapter 7.

Whatever the important social skill that causes your adolescent to have difficulties, this book can give you some direction for helping him or her improve those skills and your daily life together.

COMMUNICATION IS KEY

How can you communicate effectively with your teen in order to improve social skills?

"You always listen to us," "You don't ever get mad and yell at us," "You make it fun to learn," "You understand kids." These are some of the things that pretty tough teenagers have said to me. They say these things despite the fact that I have rules and high expectations and set definite limits. In addition, when they transgress one of my rules or fail to live within the limits established for them, I give consequences they don't like.

Much of what I do and what you can learn to do with your teenager revolves around the following six behaviors:

1. Showing respect
2. Taking your teen's needs into consideration
3. Keeping your own hostile and angry feelings under control
4. Recognizing both your child's strengths and weaknesses
5. Listening to his gripes and complaints
6. Trying (as best you can) to make it fun to learn better social skills

It is important for you to recognize that you still have a tremendous influence on your teenager. Your teen may be bigger than you or on the way there and may seem very sophisticated a lot of the time. At the same time your teen will be asking for—more likely demanding—greater freedom and autonomy from you. Yet, all adolescents still need their parents. Your teen needs a relationship with you and your continuing guidance and support. Sometimes your child may even ask for advice—although it may well be a strain for him to follow it when you give it.

SHOW RESPECT

To be in a position to teach your teen vital social skills, you need to be actively involved in your adolescent's life and to have a sound relationship. What goes into a sound relationship? It begins with the way you relate to your child, including showing her respect.

I believe that adults have to earn the respect of teenagers. One of the best ways of showing your child that you deserve respect is by showing plenty of respect for her.

This may be difficult at times, especially when your adolescent is acting in immature, irresponsible, or even silly ways. The important distinction is that you don't always have to respect your child's behavior, but you do have to respect the person. For some parents this may be a subtle difference. For instance, you can be upset and disappointed if your teenage son gets suspended from school for cutting class to be with his girlfriend. Yet it's disrespectful and counterproductive to dismiss his perceived need that led to his behavior. You can address the problem by recognizing that he felt a compelling need and by letting him know that he needs to address it in some way other than skipping classes.

Respecting your teen means that you take him seriously, that you treat his ideas and dreams as very important, and that you don't treat him with derision or disdain. In other words, deal with your teen just as you would treat another adult or colleague.

One of the reasons psychologists and psychotherapists often are successful in treating adolescents is because they demonstrate respect by taking what they say seriously and by listening to them. As parents, it's sometimes easy to see our adolescent children as disappointing or immature and to stop giving them respect.

I remember talking with Yvette, a 15-year-old girl who was having a great deal of conflict with her parents. One late August I was trying to find time for an appointment for her. I didn't have a good place in my schedule, so I told her I wasn't doing anything very important on Labor Day and I could see her then if it was okay with her.

"You mean you'd come in on a holiday to see a rotten person

like me?" she asked. She was struck by the fact that I would give up part of a holiday for her. This was obviously unique in her experience.

Yvette obviously did not have a positive self-concept because she viewed herself as a "rotten person." She was, therefore, incredulous that I would think about going out of my way for her. Demonstrating this kind of respect helped put our relationship on a solid footing. In turn, she developed more respect for me. This allowed me leverage in teaching her better communication with her parents.

RESPOND TO YOUR TEEN'S NEEDS

Most of us know that responsiveness to the needs of an infant or a young child are clearly important. Yet, I believe the need for responsiveness continues into adolescence.

Responsiveness has several elements. It means that you are loving and affectionate. It means that you show positive emotions and genuine caring and concern. Another element of responsiveness is understanding and acceptance of what your teenager needs. For most teens, those needs include acceptance, limit-setting, consistent consequences, and understanding by a caring adult. Being responsive also means being in tune with your teen's own unique needs. For example, 15-year-old Dan had been in one of my adolescent therapy groups for a short period of time. He got bored and restless easily. It was apparent that his anger was triggered when his high school teachers didn't pay attention to his restlessness. I didn't want this trait to lead to problems for the group or between him and me. One day I was explaining to his group that they couldn't always control their feelings but they could learn to control their behavior. I pointed to Dan as an example. "For instance, guys, take Dan. He's so bored right now he can hardly see straight. I know what he's thinking. He's thinking, 'When is Mr. Windell going to shut up and let us go home?' Right, Dan?" I said, asking him for confirmation.

Dan grinned and shook his head yes. Then he said, "Is it time to go yet?"

I pointed at him and said in an excited voice, "Thank you, Dan! You're terrific! That's exactly the example I needed so everyone could understand this idea. You know what, guys, Dan can't control feeling bored in here. He gets restless here just like he does in school. That's probably because I'm so boring. But did you hear what he asked me?"

"Yeah," replied Cindy, a 14-year-old girl in the group. "He said he was bored and is it time to go home."

"Right, " I said. "Very good, Cindy, you were paying attention. He's having a feeling—restlessness—and he can't control it. He can't help that. But what can he help? He can choose not to ask me to go home. He can have a bored feeling, but he doesn't have to ask every five minutes if it's time to go. Great example, Dan. You're a big help to this group."

Dan got the message, as did everyone else in the group. Admittedly, it wasn't subtle, but Dan realized he didn't have to ask so frequently if it was time to go if someone recognized that he had a high boredom factor. In groups after that session Dan raised his hand and let me know when he felt bored and restless. Instead of asking to leave, he asked if he could get up and stretch. He had learned to recognize a feeling and to make a better choice about how he would behave. I tried to be responsive to a need Dan had by recognizing it and allowing him to address it in a constructive way that did not disturb others or end his participation in the group.

KEEP YOUR ANGER UNDER CONTROL

How you handle your anger in front of your child is an important factor in building a solid relationship. That doesn't mean that you always have to be in control and that you are never allowed to show your emotions. However, losing control of your emotions can damage your relationship with your child.

The first obvious risk to losing control of your anger is that you may lose control of your words or exhibit other out-of-control behaviors. There's almost nothing that will damage your relationship more than hurtful words or comments from you.

Teenagers are often much too fragile in their identity and self-concept to tolerate a direct attack on their ego. And if the anger is loosed too often at the teen's expense, how she feels about herself and about you will suffer. How can she trust you if you can't be trusted to remain in control?

In addition, parents who give in to their anger to the extent that physical confrontations take place run the risk, first, that their teen will not want to have a relationship. The anger and resentment that teenagers feel following a slap, a spanking, or a beating by a parent make further teaching of social skills very difficult, if not impossible.

The second major risk to losing control of your anger is that your behavior belies your message that your teen needs to learn self-control and anger management. If your words say "control yourself" while your behavior very definitely says "don't control yourself," you can be sure that your child will notice the discrepancy.

A third risk in your expressing your anger too vociferously and too frequently is that your adolescent just may get used to it and tune you out. It would be a shame if your anger meant nothing to them except that you are a cranky, unpredictable person to be avoided. Then, you have lost the ability to use your anger in strategic and positive ways.

With my own children and with the teenagers in my groups, I like to have my anger mean something; that is, when I show anger, it should have greater impact on them than just that the old man blew a fuse again. If you ask my children today how many times they saw me angry when they were growing up, they would probably say I never got angry. But when pressed, they can remember a few instances when I lost it and let them know that I was really mad. The same thing happens in my groups with teenagers. I am generally calm, easygoing, and predictable. But on the rare occasions when I get truly mad at one or more people in the group, I want them to know it and for it to be unmistakable. Therefore, a couple of times a year, I will let my anger show, usually by using an angry voice or slamming my hand down on a table.

You can be sure that after coming to expect a relatively soft-spoken and rarely upset person, the kids will sit up and take notice when I get angry. These kids often come from homes where there is much violence and anger. Dealing with an angry parent is an everyday occurrence for most of them. But when I get angry, it is an event, and they listen up. After it's over and for the next couple of weeks, teens will talk about the day Mr. Windell got angry.

"You should have been here," one kid will say to another who wasn't at that session. "Mr. Windell got so mad. He said words he never said before."

The most important thing that should come out of one of these episodes when I express my anger is that the adolescents realize I have limits and won't allow them to walk all over me. If they push me too far, I'll get mad. But they can predict this and they know I won't hold a grudge. In fact, we always talk about it later. If I feel I've gone a bit too far, I always apologize, explain why I got so mad, and tell how this can be avoided in the future.

In contrast to my behavior, Joanne, a single mother of 15-year-old Kevin, more frequently loses control of her anger. While she and Kevin generally get along well and Joanne is a competent, loving parent, sometimes she feels a lot of pressure at work just at the time Kevin pushes her limits too far. That's when she loses it. For example, Kevin once brought home a report card on which he had two failing marks after assuring her all marking period that he was studying hard and that she had no reason to be concerned.

"You lied to me and I can't trust you," she yelled at Kevin. "I can see you're nothing more than a little child who has to be treated like a baby. I'll have to check your homework each night and call your teachers once a week to see to it that you aren't lying to me. What you've done to me is disgusting, and I don't even want to look at you anymore! There's nothing I hate worse than liars!"

Kevin was flabbergasted by his mother's explosion of rage. He was also hurt by what she said. He had thought he was more mature than most 15-year-olds, so her criticism rocked his sense of who he was. He went angrily to his room and vowed to himself he would never talk to her again. When he talked about this incident with an uncle, he complained that his mother never gave him a chance to explain his side of the low grades.

When Joanne cooled down and thought about how she had handled the situation, she knew she had hurt him and damaged their relationship because she attacked him personally. She knew she had to repair the damage she did, but she didn't know if Kevin could forgive her or if they would be able to start over and talk about the real issue of the low grades in a more reasonable way.

A few days later, she found an opportunity to apologize to Kevin. "I'm sorry for going off on you about your grades. I didn't mean what I said, and I don't think you're immature or that I have to treat you like a child. I'm sorry I said those things."

While Kevin listened, he was not ready to forgive her. It took him several more days of thinking about it before he remembered that she really loved him and probably had a right to be mad about his grades. When he did reopen the discussion, he asked her to do him a favor. "Would you think about what you're going to say before you yell at me? That way you won't get so mad and I won't feel so much hatred toward you."

Joanne readily agreed to avoid a repeat of this incident, and the two were finally able to work on a plan for Kevin to bring up his grades.

RECOGNIZE AND ENCOURAGE THEIR STRENGTHS

Perhaps even more important than recognizing and accepting your adolescent's weaknesses is recognizing and encouraging her strengths.

Teenagers, while trying to figure out who they are, need help in discovering their strengths, assets, and good points. Knowing yourself is a key in learning to like and appreciate who you are. Pointing out your teen's assets inevitably helps your child through the sometimes confusing process of developing into an adult with a strong sense of personal identity.

Too often I find parents of teens get hung up on the problems, the faults, the breaking of rules, and the irritating behaviors, fads, and manners of adolescents, and they pay far too little attention to the positives. Although constructive criticism might be useful at times, all it teaches a teenager is what he should avoid or change. Important as that is, it does not tell him what he will be good at, what he will enjoy, and what he can do better than others. Certainly, teens are likely to hear enough from many sources about what they aren't doing so well.

Focusing on your child's good traits, characteristics, and strengths will also help him begin to formulate some ideas of what he's going to do with his life.

This is the age where he needs to start thinking about where he's going, what he's going to do for a career, and how he's going to fit into this world. If he knows what he's good at, then he has an edge in settling on a path toward success and happiness.

Fifteen-year-old Christine may be good at listening to problems and caring for others who have problems, which might mean she could be a doctor, nurse, or psychologist. Sixteen-year-old Steven causes his parents concern because he spends too much of his time on the computer. Yet, he has a gift for understanding how computers work, and I suspect he will work in some capacity with computers when he's older.

RECOGNIZE AND ACCEPT THEIR WEAKNESSES

All young people have weaknesses as well as strengths and assets. And most adolescents know what their weak points are. I find that even delinquent adolescents who are generally not known for their insight have a good sense of what their weaknesses and failings are.

How you handle those weaknesses is critical if you want to achieve a strong relationship with your teenager. If you take the position that you must point out your child's weaknesses and make frequent references to them, you are likely to damage the relationship and cause resentment.

Discussing weaknesses and self-defeating behaviors, as you will see more clearly in Chapter 3, is important in teaching teens social skills. But it does not mean that you must sit in judgment, frequently pointing out their faults and urging changes. Because adolescents are in the phase of development when they are attempting to establish who they are and to form a solid self-concept, they will not usually handle criticism very well.

Your job is to understand your child's failings and accept her weaknesses. You don't have to point them out or give lectures on why and how they should be changed. Accepting your adolescent's weaknesses only means that you know her trouble spots and that you accept that those are *her* trouble spots, which you will help her change when she's ready. In the meantime, you can look for golden opportunities to help her get ready or to have more insight into what her weak areas are.

For example, Christine's father worried about her because she had several teenage friends who used alcohol and drugs. He wanted to lecture her about how her friends' reputation would reflect on her reputation and how they could possibly influence her to begin using drugs or alcohol. He refrained from doing this though, as he tried to understand her motivation in having those friends.

One Saturday night when Christine was at a party, she called her dad and asked him to come and help her get another girl home who was too drunk to function on her own. He drove to the party and helped Christine take her friend home. As they were themselves returning home, he commented to Christine about his appreciation of her concern for her friends.

"If I didn't help these kids," Christine said, "they wouldn't have anyone to take care of them."

Her father immediately saw the piece of the puzzle that had been missing. Christine had a collection of friends who needed someone to look after them and help them out. While he decided that there were some risks in Christine assuming this role, he saw that she wasn't as likely to emulate their behavior as she was to just be available to help them. He knew he could deal with this at another place and time. But he also knew he would have to be gentle and caring in broaching the subject of these friends.

Another parent might have criticized Christine's choice of friends or attacked her decision to go to a party where there were alcohol and drugs. To do so, though, would have been to miss the point of why she had friends "with broken wings" (as her father characterized it) and might have led to a serious breakdown in their relationship.

Accepting negative qualities does not mean liking them. It means that you understand and see what the weak areas are. You don't applaud them, you just accept them being there. If you can help your teen feel better about them or work with him to change them, you will. But you won't reject your child for having them or make his life miserable because of them. This should also be considered a part of the respect that I mentioned before.

LISTEN TO THEIR GRIPES

As a responsive parent you will listen to whatever feelings and thoughts your kid expresses. However, a special part of being a responsive parent is listening to a kid's complaints and gripes. And because this is so important, I wanted to bring it to your attention in a different way and to highlight it with examples and illustrations.

Diana Baumrind, a researcher in parenting at the University of California at Berkeley, talks about the "reciprocity" that has to exist between parent and child—the extent to which parents take into account their child's wishes and feelings. Baumrind points out that her studies find that reciprocity generates prosocial behavior and that it is a factor in obtaining a child's compliance.

What this really means is that when a parent cooperates with a child—by listening, by trying to deal with complaints, and by understanding feelings and gripes—the child's willingness to cooperate with the parent is enhanced. So when you're listening to a teenager's complaints and gripes "about the way things are done around here," you're doing more than lending an ear. You're actually enhancing his ability and willingness to cooperate with you and other adults.

I've always found in working with adolescents that when they raise an issue and I treat it seriously, even if I can't exactly change the problem they have, there's a special sense of closeness that develops and increases between us in the future. In addition, it tends to deflate their complaint.

For instance, a frequent complaint I get in my social skills training groups is that the videos I show them to illustrate points about peer pressure, violence, or anger management aren't realistic or that they are, to use the word of one particular teen who was in one of my groups, "cheesy." Whenever a young person brings this up, I listen respectfully and then I say something like, "You know you're right and I really appreciate your thoughtfulness in bringing this to my attention. I've tried to find the best and most interesting training videos possible. But you know what, you could be a big help. Would you be willing to help me preview some videos I'm considering for my groups? I think you have a special interest in this, and your opinion would be valuable to me."

Sometimes they actually do help out. More often, they grudgingly agree but don't follow up. But even then, they know that I have taken their gripe seriously and that I am willing to listen to any problem they have. That is disarming to oppositional teens who expect adults to be unresponsive.

TAKE THE BOREDOM OUT OF TEACHING

It's one thing to try to teach lessons to teenagers. It's another thing to make the lesson so wearisome and boring that kids are turned off. *How* you try to teach a lesson is as important as *what* you're trying to teach.

This basically means that as a parent you have to be concerned about how you go about teaching a lesson. Each of us has many teachers during our lifetime. But how many of those truly make an impact on us? And of those who do, which are the ones that lead us to learn the lessons they are trying to teach us?

Most of us remember the teachers who seemed to like us—they're teachers who have the ability to make their lessons fascinating. They are able to get across lessons with interest, fascination, and student involvement. And as a parent, you should be aiming to be that kind of teacher to your child.

How do you best do that? Based on my own experience with my children and with the adolescents I try to teach, there are three essential ways to make lessons memorable:

1. Make sure you convey a deep and abiding interest in your child.

2. Make sure you teach with passion and fire.

3. Make sure that you teach what your child wants to know.

Make Sure You Convey a Deep and Abiding Interest in Your Child

Your teen has to know that you believe in and accept her, that you care about her and what happens to her, and that she is very important to you. If young people believe that you have their interest at heart, they are more likely to listen to what you have to say.

Fifteen-year-old Paula's parents are teachers. A big conflict in the family is Paula's parents' emphasis on the importance of grades. To Paula it seems that they place far more importance on the value of grades than they do on the value of learning. For this reason, almost anything they say about her grades ends up with Paula tuning them out or getting into an argument with them. She knows they love her, but she has stopped believing that they are encouraging good grades to help her. In fact, Paula believes they are working out some of their own problems, like reliving their own student experiences and pushing her toward a kind of success they never had. The value of what they could be teaching her about hard work and sacrifice at school is, therefore, lost.

Make Sure You Teach with Passion and Fire

It's one thing to have knowledge about a subject; it's another thing to be able to teach it with a feeling of passion that comes across to students. I think teenagers are looking for adults who truly believe and practice what they preach. That kind of commitment, which they often find lacking in adults, is important. The excesses and the passions that teenagers feel have often burned out in adults. When kids see the fires burning, though, they recognize it and are willing to pay attention to it.

The last thing they need is a teacher who is lukewarm about the subject or is hypocritical. To effectively teach your child, it is important that your passion for a subject shine through—whether it's goal-setting, anger control, or abstinence from alcohol or drugs. Teenagers get turned off by a parent or an adult who is going through the motions and teaching a subject because it is "what parents are supposed to do."

Make Sure that You Teach What Your Child Wants to Know

You have to connect somehow. Your teen has to want the information you are imparting. That means it is vital that you somehow make it practical and useful.

When your teen asks you a question or hints around about something, you have a potential hook. For example, when I'm teaching anger management methods, teens typically ask, "Why do we have to learn about deep breathing? How's this going to help us if somebody is threatening us?"

I know this question isn't asked out of idle curiosity or just to be difficult. They truly want to know. That gives me a great opportunity to answer the question and to teach a brief lesson about which anger management methods will be useful in specific situations.

USE A MULTIMEDIA LESSON IF POSSIBLE

Just talking is not always good enough. Try to make lessons more interesting and more memorable by using different teaching mechanisms.

While watching a movie with your teen, discuss the actions of the hero and of other characters and talk about how they could have handled situations differently. Discuss the morality of the characters and why they did or did not do the right thing.

If you can find videos designed to teach social skills (see suggestions in Resources at end of book), use them to help teach lessons to your teen. Engage your child in role-playing, or, as a family project, write a play or short skit.

Leave notes, quotes, or ideas on a family bulletin board or write ideas on a dry erase board. Occasionally give your teen a copy of an inspirational article, essay, or book. As much as possible, teach through different media. Not all adolescents learn in the same way, so if you can teach your child through appealing to different senses, there is a better chance he will remember the lesson you're trying to teach.

GOLDEN OPPORTUNITIES FOR LESSONS

Very often, in day-to-day life with your teenager, "golden opportunities" for lessons will arise. These are situations that present themselves that give you a special chance to teach a lesson. Take advantage of these. Here's an example. One day when I was driving my children somewhere, my daughter, in middle school at the time, said, "There's a girl in my school who has a bottle of vodka in her locker."

Certainly I was concerned, and I recognized this as one of those teachable moments when she was clearly interested in what I had to say about a classmate having a bottle of vodka in her locker. I started by asking Jill a question. "What do you think about someone who is drinking vodka at school?"

"I think she's dumb," my daughter said.

"Why?" I asked.

"Because she could get in big trouble," Jill replied.

"Is that the only reason you think it's dumb?" I said.

"No," Jill said. "How can she learn anything or do her work if she's drunk? She's going to flunk out of school if she keeps that up."

"Yes," I said, "I really agree with you. Drinking alcohol is a dangerous thing to do. She can't do well in school or in friendships if she's drinking. But there's something else that concerns me."

"What's that?" Jill asked.

I told her, "If she's hiding vodka in her locker and drinking during the day, that probably means she has problems she's not able to share with others. For instance, she's not talking to her parents about whatever is bothering her. That's too bad that she can't do that. I'm sure her parents would like to help her out. No matter what's bothering her, I would hope that her parents could talk to her about it and help her find a way to handle it."

"I'll bet they'd be mad if they knew she was drinking vodka," Jill said.

"Maybe," I said. "But they might be relieved if she came and talked to them and told them she was drinking and asked for their help."

"Yeah," said Jill.

That was the end of that conversation. Whether Jill can re-member this conversation or others like it, I'm not sure. What I do know is that it is now more than fifteen years since this discussion took place and she has never had a drinking problem. I certainly can't take all the credit for this, but I'd like to think that how golden opportunities like this were handled have played a part in some of her life decisions.

Jill's initial statement about a girl at school presented one of those situations that doesn't come along often enough with our children, but when they do, you want to take advantage of them. That's what makes it a golden opportunity. It's like someone sug-gesting you buy an unknown stock called Microsoft in 1981. Take advantage of a golden opportunity, and you'll profit from it for a long time. Fail to use it, and you'll kick yourself afterward.

Always be on the lookout for those golden opportunities. You can usually recognize them because your teen will be asking a question. Golden opportunity questions may sound like this:

"What's so bad about smoking marijuana?"
"Why do I have to go to college?"
"What difference does it make if I learn geometry? I'll never use it."
"What was it like when you went to high school?"
"What's the big deal about teenagers having sex?"
"Why do I have to go to church?"
"Did you ever use drugs?"

These are questions you may be tempted to answer with a flip-pant remark or with a lecture. Resist any initial temptations to give your opinion, and first find out where he or she stands on the issue and what the question means for him or her.

Then there are comments or statements that provide golden opportunities, too. They often come about like this:

"A girl at school is pregnant."

"One of the guys on the football team says that steroids won't hurt you."

"The substitute teacher made some racist comments."

"Jermaine said his father cheats on his income tax and never gets caught."

"Hillary's parents don't care how late she stays out."

"Karen's mother gets mad so easily."

"I got my progress report today."

"A kid at school showed me how to get into the school's computer system."

Then, too, there are golden opportunity situations. These can include TV shows that have a theme that can open up conversations and discussions. Plays and movies can do the same thing. Walking in on your child who is chatting on the Internet and using obscene language is a golden opportunity. So is finding out that your teenager has ordered a pay-for-view, X-rated TV movie. Each time you are with your adolescent in public, you can probably find at least one, if not several, golden opportunities.

I remember one time when my son Jason played a cassette tape for me in the car one day. I had not heard this group before and he asked me to listen to this "cool" group he had discovered. After listening for a while, I had a golden opportunity to say something about what I believe about sexually explicit audio tapes and antiwomen messages. What I said was that I had trouble with some of the lyrics I heard: "You may think some of these lyrics are funny or clever, but think about what they say about women. Would you feel comfortable playing this tape in front of your mother or a girl you respected? If you wouldn't, then you have to ask yourself why you are listening to this group and their lyrics."

Another time, my daughter was with me at an outdoor jazz concert. The smell of marijuana was wafting through the air and she asked what that strange smell was. After answering, I had an opportunity to make an editorial comment about drug use. "You might as well get used to this smell," I said, "because you will come across it again. You'll see kids using marijuana at school and at parties, and they'll probably offer you some. You'll probably be tempted to try it."

"I wouldn't do that," she said.

"I know you think that now," I said, "but most of us are tempted to try things that other people say make them feel good. I'm not in favor of people using any drugs. I would prefer that you read as much as you can about drugs and what effects they can have on you. And always be aware that no matter how much you trust the person who is urging you to try something, you don't really know what it is you're trying or where it came from."

HELP THEM LEARN THEIR OWN LESSONS

Many times parents miss out on golden opportunities by using a sledge hammer to get their lesson across. They either do this by making the lesson too obvious or by constantly repeating it when the original point was made long ago.

Many parents believe that important lessons must be delivered in a stern or serious voice, must be given in a long lecture, or must have a moral. If you give lectures that are too long, too boring, too formal, or too preachy, your child will tune out and you will fail to teach when an opportunity existed.

You can teach an important social skills lesson in one sentence, one joke, or one short, pithy story. For example, a friend of mine once told me that when he was in high school, he told a teacher he liked about his desire to be a lawyer. "The world doesn't need any more regular lawyers," she said. "But the world is in need of good, ethical lawyers."

My friend went on to be an attorney who served on ethics panels for lawyers. In two sentences, his teacher taught him a lesson that he never forgot.

REINFORCE LESSONS

Don't forget to use old-fashioned praise and rewards sometimes to punctuate the importance of what your teen is learning or how well he has remembered a social skill.

Just because he's a teenager doesn't mean that rewards and motivations won't still be useful. I find that even sophisticated and hard-core teenagers, kids who are blase about a lot in life, are still often thrilled by a well-placed "nice going" or a simple reward, such as a gift certificate to a favorite fast-food restaurant or a certificate I made on my computer.

Of course, rewards shouldn't be overused or viewed as a substitute for your interest and involvement. Those are still the most important things you have to offer.

PART TWO

SIX SKILLS TO TEACH YOUR TEEN

2

STEP ONE: TEACH YOUR TEENAGER TO SET GOALS

R ay was a big, burly teenager who showed up in one of my groups wearing a hood that covered his head and much of his face. He had several days' growth of beard, and instead of talking he snarled and mumbled.

The day he appeared was a day we were working on goals. I asked him to identify some of his goals.

"I don't got any," he said with a venomous hiss.

"You don't?" I said, feigning surprise. I had been through this many times with teens over the past several years. I know most of the adolescents I work with don't have clear goals for their life.

"Nah," he said. "What do I need goals for? I live from day to day."

"So you haven't actually set any personal goals," I said. "Most of the kids I work with have never set any goals for themselves. But, if you don't know where you're going, that's where you're going to end up—nowhere."

Ray seemed unfazed by my delivery of that line. It's one of my favorite lines. I use it because I hope it sinks in with teenagers and because I also happen to think it's true. People who don't plan or identify goals for themselves will live haphazard lives not fully using the abilities, talents, skills, and potentials that they have. Like the main character in the film *Good Will Hunting,* an adolescent may be blessed with great ability but may not use it (20-year-old Will Hunting was a genius in mathematics, in case you haven't seen the movie). Will's goals in life were very short term and were not planned around his extraordinary mathematical abilities. Instead, he worked as a janitor with no apparent goal to get an education and use it. So many adolescents, like Will, have not developed the self-discipline of setting goals and having a roadmap for the future. As a consequence, their journey through life may be full of painful roadblocks and plenty of detours.

Many of the adolescents I tend to see are very impulsive and live more for the moment rather than planning for the long term. But living for the moment with its spontaneity—while perhaps more exciting—is not in their long-term interests. That's what goals are all about—charting the future. Without plans and a chart, teenagers will end up somewhere, perhaps adrift in a sea of never-realized potential, but probably not at a rewarding journey's end.

Setting goals and working hard to attain them is a big part of maturity.

I know we all want our children to accomplish something important and satisfying in the future. We can exhort them to study hard and to attain things, but unless we teach them *how* to do this, they won't know what to do today to accomplish their dreams or visions. And we'll wonder why they didn't accomplish what they were capable of.

If you've never tried to teach your adolescent to set goals, you may be confused as to where to begin. That's what we'll cover here. I'll also explain some of the difficulties you'll likely encounter and explain some of the tools I've developed to help teens set and stick to some important goals.

A FEW THINGS TO KEEP IN MIND
ABOUT SETTING GOALS

If you haven't taught your teenager this valuable social skill, you are likely to encounter resistance. In fact because high school students tend to want to control their own destiny, your child may actually be downright hostile to the idea. Many kids don't want anyone spoiling their fun and the spontaneous nature of their day-to-day routine. So be sure you approach this in a positive way, and plan to be persistent. I cannot overemphasize the importance of this. As you can imagine, some of the teens to whom I try to teach goal-setting, like Ray, don't want anyone changing their life. They are tough, past masters at being oppositional and resistant. But what you're also teaching by example is to be persistent. If teens are going to reach challenging goals in life, they're going to need plenty of persistence. So don't give up easily just because they don't jump at the idea of learning to set goals.

You could start out by saying something like, "You really started to do well at the end of the last school year. I'd like to make sure you keep your momentum going. How about if we talk about some goals for this school year?"

Be prepared for your teen to roll her eyes and resist or perhaps humor you. "Sure, Dad. Listen I promised Debby I'd be at her house. So I'll talk to you later about this." Then she's gone.

Keep your positive and encouraging demeanor and attitude. Try something like this: "I know this sounds like something you don't want to do or need. But many successful people your age and older set goals for themselves. I think you'll find that this will help you focus your energies at school this year. Let's try it anyway, okay? How about at nine o'clock tonight when you get back from Debby's?"

Setting a time and not letting them wiggle out of it is an important strategy. Keep at it until a time is nailed down.

Use questions and even tasks as part of the process. Encourage your teen to think of two or three problems she had at school last year, or of two things that went wrong during the last basketball season, or three things she would like to improve in her social relationships this year. Get her thinking in terms of problems. Then move from the problems to how she could change, improve, erase, or decrease previous problems and difficulties. That automatically means she is setting goals.

Many teens, while they might not come straight out and oppose you by refusing to engage in this process, will try to find ways of avoiding doing anything serious with goals. For instance, your child may come up with some quick, broad goals. "I'd like to get better grades and stay out of trouble with my teachers. Okay, satisfied?"

Those broad goals aren't specific enough to do much good. Therefore, you've got to ask more questions. "What do you mean, you want to do better in your classes?" Have her spell out exactly what she wants to accomplish in each class. Does she want to complete all assignments and turn them in on time? Would she like to be more proficient on exams? Would she like to achieve Bs in history and English? Would just passing be a reasonable goal? Is a 4.0 average for the year the most challenging but still attainable goal? These decisions can only be made after you've asked questions and done some probing.

All goals must be reasonable and attainable. Setting high goals is important, but if the goals are so high that your child could not realistically reach them, it would be discouraging and perhaps self-defeating. If a teenager hasn't played on a basketball team before, it is unrealistic for him to expect he will make the varsity squad as a starter. If she has been a loner without friends, it may be a real stretch to think that she will be the president of the Student Council. Intermediate steps make much more sense.

When I was helping 14-year-old Patrick, who was a loner without friends most of his life, we began with some small goals. The first steps were for him to smile at three or four kids each day. Then to say hello to one person a day. After several weeks, we graduated to Patrick asking a classmate for his phone number to call him at home about school work. This helped him develop some friendships. After several months, he was ready to deal with bullies who picked on him. We could never have started there.

HOW PARENTS CAN TEACH GOAL-SETTING

I was talking to a teenager from Syracuse, New York, recently. She told me about talking to her mother while in the eleventh grade about the colleges she would apply to and what course of study she planned to pursue.

"We both agreed," 17-year-old Sarah said, "that I was outgoing and I liked people. She thought I might like something in personnel work."

At the time, Sarah thought it was a good idea, and her mother and she further agreed that getting a job at a local Holiday Inn might help out. She began working there and within a few months got the job of pool manager.

"The more I worked there," Sarah explained, "the more I loved working in the motel. So I talked to my mother, and we came up with hotel and motel management as a career goal. I'm really excited to go to college because I'm sure that's what I want to do."

In this case, Sarah was not only engaged in goal-setting, she was also giving herself, with the encouragement of her mother, the opportunity for more experiences. As is clear with Sarah, choosing a career doesn't need to take place in a vacuum. Talking to adults, as Sarah did with her mother, and having new experiences often lead to revisions in original goals.

rah's mother didn't have to formally teach Sarah how to set goals and plan because they had a good relationship and Sarah respects her mother's advice. However, you may want to have a format in mind in order to better teach your teen how to go about setting goals. I use this four-step method in teaching teenagers about goal-setting:

1. Identify your goals.
2. Brainstorm ways to accomplish these goals. Use the best ideas to design an action plan.
3. Take the first step.
4. Evaluate your goals and action plan periodically, and make changes when necessary.

GETTING YOUR TEEN
TO IDENTIFY GOALS

Identifying goals is not always easy for adolescents. It's not even so easy for mature adults. Sometimes we're caught in a transitional phase as we move from one part of adulthood to another. We're just not sure what we want to do with some parts of our life. It could be that we are making a transition in our marriage or love life, in our career, in our family life, in our social life, or in our geographic location.

Well, the fact is that that is what adolescence is all about— making one big transition. So for a teen to pin down some exact goals may be very difficult. Your job is to help him or her do some serious thinking about this. Sarah was approaching the end of high school, the time when she would have to make some decisions about college. She herself had, as I think many teenagers have, some worries and concerns about what would come after high school.

I've already said that you are likely to invite resistance by doing this, but even if your child is cooperative and senses a need to set goals, she may not know quite what she wants out of life. You can help by asking the right questions. Here is a list of questions I've used that gets teens thinking about their goals:

- What career appeals most to you?

- Where do you think you'd like to be in five (or three, or two, or one) years?

- What would you like to change about your life?

- What would you like to accomplish at school in the next semester?

- Are you satisfied with your friendships? Anything you would like to change about your social relationships?

- What would you like to do for fun or a hobby this year?

- What gets you into the most trouble that you'd like to do something about?

- What is there about yourself that you'd like to have different?

- What are some of your behaviors you'd like to change?

- What changes would you like to work on in our family?

Usually, like other parts of this process, identifying goals is a brainstorming activity. Your questions can help set the brain activity in motion. I have found that even the most difficult and resistant teenager has some goals—such as to get off probation or to stop getting caught by the police or even to get away from me permanently!

While some young people could identify five or ten goals, it's best to settle on a smaller number—say three or four. That allows them to devote more time and attention to the goals selected. Here are some reasonable goals teenagers in my groups have set:

- To stop smoking

- To get all passing grades

- To have a better relationship with my mother

- To get a job so I can help support my family

- To get all Bs or above in school so I can go to college

- To stop using drugs

- To do community service with the homeless

- To make the first string on the varsity football team

- To learn to control my temper

- To learn all I can about computers

- To be in the school jazz band

My experience has been that with a little prodding, a lot of patience, and considerable perseverance your teenager will identify several goals important to him.

BRAINSTORMING FOR IDEAS TO DEVELOP A PLAN OF ACTION

Once a few goals have been identified, the next step is to brainstorm ideas about how those goals can be reached.

One teenager I know could identify that she had a problem with her temper. When I asked her to brainstorm ideas about how she could control her temper, she came up with one idea: Don't get mad.

"That sounds like a good idea," I said, "but how are you going to go through the rest of your life without getting mad?"

"I won't let anything bother me," she replied.

"But how are you going to do that?" I persisted.

"I don't know," she said, "I guess I'll just try hard."

"Sorry," I said. "That's not good enough. Tell me exactly how you are going to work at controlling your temper."

She sputtered for a moment and finally said, "I'll walk away if someone is making me mad."

"Hey, now you're talking," I said enthusiastically. "You're starting to brainstorm ideas. Come up with a few more of those kinds of ideas and you'll be on your way to developing a plan of action."

This dialogue gives you a sense of how to handle this stage of the process. Many adolescents want to give a quick, easy response and are reluctant to truly brainstorm ideas that lend themselves to an action plan that will further their efforts to reach a goal. Many teenagers aren't used to brainstorming ideas. That's where your patience, prodding, and persistence again come into play.

Don't let your teen off the hook by accepting a facile answer or thought. Allowing him to come up with simplistic and overgeneralized ideas means he doesn't really have to think. But thinking is exactly what you want him to do—to think about his goals and to come up with many different ideas.

Remember that the essence of brainstorming is that no one criticize any ideas, at least not at first. Sometimes adding some encouragement can prime the pump of a teen's creative brain. You can say things like, "Yes, good start—that's one idea, what's another?" or "That really sounds like you're on the right track" or even, "That's creative. Try for another one. Don't think too much. Just let the ideas flow."

Hopefully for every goal, your child can come up with five or six, maybe even ten workable ideas that will enable her to put together a plan of action. After brainstorming, she should have several ideas that are worthwhile and can go in an action plan. Others may seem unhelpful or superficial.

Amanda decided that one of her major goals was to get along better with her mother. Amanda has diabetes, and her apparent reluctance to check her blood-sugar levels regularly was an issue that frequently led to arguments between them. When she was brainstorming ideas to accomplish this goal, she came up with the following ideas:

- Stop fighting with Mom.
- Listen to her when she tells me to do something.
- Let her criticism go in one ear and out the other.
- Don't get in arguments with her.
- Ignore her when she yells at me.
- Get better grades.
- Come home on time.
- Clean my room at least once a week.
- Check my blood-sugar levels regularly, and watch my diet.
- Don't swear at her even if I get mad.

Having come up with all of these ideas, she needed to condense or combine some of them as well as to pick out the ones that were most important. In developing an action plan, she settled on three things that would improve the relationship:

1. Check my blood-sugar levels four times a day and record them so that Mom can check them any time she's worried.
2. Clean my room once a week.
3. Improve my school grades so that I have a B average.

These three actions she could take constituted a viable action plan for Amanda. What she then had to do was to plan to take the first step toward her goal of improving her relationship with her mother.

TAKING THE FIRST STEP

Taking the first step is the most essential as well as the most exciting thing a teen can do when starting out to reach a goal. No goal will ever be successful if your adolescent can't agree on a first step and take it. So, after the goal has been identified and the action plan has been put together, a logical question can be: What will you do first?

For Amanda, whose diabetes is a life-threatening disease, what she will do to check her blood-sugar levels will be critical—both to her and to her mother. Amanda decided that her first step, which she could begin the next day, was to begin by checking her blood-sugar levels and recording the data at 6:45 A.M., just after getting up for school. She would also check her blood sugars three additional times each day.

She also decided that during the first week of her plan, she could clean her room on Saturday morning and bring home schoolwork every day to complete. She set an estimated time frame of three months to accomplish her goal of a better mother-daughter relationship.

EVALUATING THE PLAN

An evaluation of a plan to reach a goal can be done at any time. But it makes sense to set a date for an assessment of how the action plan is working.

You can be involved in this evaluation with your teen. She

may need a reminder to do an evaluation, or you may see at some point that an evaluation is in order. This could be because she is not progressing toward a goal or has become discouraged by the difficulty of it or because it has become apparent (at least to you) that the goal is impractical.

In evaluating a goal, a teen must face these questions:

- How am I doing with my action plan?
- Am I getting closer to my goal?
- Does it look like I can meet my goal by my arbitrary deadline?
- Is my goal one I can really reach?
- Should anything be changed about this goal, for instance, the plan of action or the deadline?

After answering these questions and making any necessary alterations in the goal or plan of action, it is necessary to move on. The importance of this cannot be overemphasized.

Some teenagers, given any setbacks or difficulties meeting a goal, will get discouraged or become so disappointed with themselves that they will give up. As a parent you can offer encouragement and be a cheering section to help your teen see beyond any temporary setbacks. He will need to keep focused on the long-range goal and the final outcome—which based on the goal-setting process should be within his reach. But he has to persevere to reach the goal. You want to be in the position of giving him a boost to get over the hump of discouragement and disappointment so he will be ultimately successful.

No matter what, your message should be to evaluate where your child is in relation to the goal, to make any necessary alterations, and to move on with a sense of purpose and determination. The earlier an adolescent learns this lesson in life, the better chance he will have to be successful as an adult.

GOLDEN OPPORTUNITIES TO TEACH GOAL-SETTING

When it comes to setting goals and striving to reach those goals, life in a family is full of golden opportunities. Whether it's a parent's personal goals at work, family goals, or the goals of one of the children in the family, you have plenty of chances to show teenagers the importance of the goal-setting process.

For example, if one of the children in the family decides that she will try to make the swim team at school, you could use this as an opportunity to teach everyone—especially your teenager—about setting a goal and working to achieve it. You could say, "Let's all try to figure out what Cynthia has to do in order to make the swim team." When others are invited to join in the process, they get a chance to brainstorm ideas, to make suggestions, and to watch you guide your child to identify her goals, make a plan of action, and decide what her first steps will be.

Or let's say that the family wants to take a summer vacation to Disney World. Talk about setting goals for the trip (planning the itinerary, saving the money, deciding on a time, getting airline tickets, and so on). Discuss how everyone's working together can make it a reality.

You don't have to be heavy-handed about pointing out that your adolescent should learn from the process and apply it to his life. If he is involved he will be learning a process—whether he intends to be learning or not.

When my daughter was a young adolescent, we decided to start a company to publish mental health pamphlets. I talked to Jill frequently about my plans and goals and how I planned to reach those goals. She was aware of the concern about raising money, selling products, and establishing a distribution system. Throughout her adolescent years, I gradually brought her more and more into the planning and goal-setting so she had a good idea about what was involved in starting a company and how one worked hard to reach certain goals.

One of the things my daughter learned from this (and I'm sure from other opportunities to watch her family set goals and strive to reach them) was that she could set major goals and work hard to attain them. As she has matured into an adult, I watched with fascination as she saved to buy her first house and thought about her own business opportunities. I believe the goal-setting and planning she witnessed as a child and adolescent helped her in her life. She recently started her own business, and I have no doubt that because of careful planning she will be successful.

PUTTING IT INTO ACTION

You can use this goal-setting worksheet with your teen either by having him or her fill it out or by reading the statements and questions aloud and filling it out together.

GOAL-SETTING WORKSHEET

A. *Identify Your Goals:*

    1. What things are really important to you to do in the next six months? List below some of the things you would like to do in the next six months:

        a.

        b.

        c.

        d.

        e.

        f.

        g.

2. Now look at the list, and circle the top one or two Goals.

3. Think about behaviors or actions of yours that could stop you from or get in the way of achieving one or more important Goals. Write your most serious Self-Defeating Behaviors here:

    a.

    b.

    c.

B. *Brainstorm, and Make a Plan of Action:*

    Write down as many ideas as you can for each of your Goals.

    1. My ideas to reach Goal Number One:

        a.

        b.

        c.

        d.

        e.

    2. My ideas to reach Goal Number Two:

        a.

        b.

        c.

        d.

        e.

C. *Take the First Step:*

    For each of your Goals, write down your plan of action and the first step you will take, beginning tomorrow:

    1. My Plan of Action to Reach Goal Number One:

        a. My Plan of Action will be to do the following things:

      (1)

      (2)

      (3)

      (4)

      (5)

  b. The first step I will take tomorrow to begin to try to reach this Goal is: _____ .

  c. Other things I will do this week to begin working at this Goal are:

      (1)

      (2)

      (3)

  d. I plan to reach this goal by this date: _____ .

2. My Plan of Action to Reach Goal Number Two:

  a. My Plan of Action will be to do the following things:

      (1)

      (2)

      (3)

      (4)

      (5)

  b. The first step I will take tomorrow to begin to try to reach this Goal is: _____ .

  c. Other things I will do this week to begin working at this Goal are:

      (1)

      (2)

      (3)

  d. I plan to reach this Goal by this date: _____ .

3

STEP TWO: TEACH YOUR TEENAGER TO IDENTIFY AND CHANGE SELF-DEFEATING BEHAVIORS

Step One involved setting goals. But what stands in the way of your teen reaching a goal? Usually only one thing: himself or herself . . . at least that's what motivational speakers say. I tend to believe this. But I like to specifically look at what it is about oneself that gets in the way of accomplishing an important goal.

It is self-defeating behaviors that stop us from reaching our goals. Self-defeating behaviors can be anything—from the use of alcohol or drugs, to depression, laziness, anger, or jealousy—that keeps us from improving. A lot of the behaviors I choose to call self-defeating, other people might see as a psychiatric or physical illness. Things like alcoholism, depression, attention deficit disorder, drug addiction, frequent rages, or moodiness might be called disorders or syndromes. However, when we view the actions and behaviors that interfere with goal attainment as something outside of our control, then we have a built-in excuse for not doing anything about it.

When I work with teenagers, whether they are delinquent or just kids who haven't lived up to their potential or to the expec-

53

tations others have for them, I hear them give all sorts of excuses and reasons why they cannot accomplish their goals.

"What do you expect?" one teen said to me. "I've got attention deficit disorder. I can't pay attention in school."

Another adolescent recently said to me, "Sure, I'd like to get a good job, but I have dyslexia, and I can't fill out an application form."

Another one said that she would like to do better at school. "But," she said, "I've always been lazy."

When kids have grown up believing they have had a disorder or problem, they sometimes feel they can avoid taking responsibility for their life and their actions. But I don't want to let them get away with this because they are the ones who lose out. When I challenge their excuses, I am constantly amazed at how much they can accomplish and how goals that they thought were unattainable suddenly come within reach.

While I'm aware that disorders, illnesses, and "conditions" do exist, I prefer to see the challenges raised by them as detours rather than roadblocks. I don't want adolescents to make excuses and find reasons why they can't do something. I'd rather have them brainstorm and find all the ways in which they can overcome their areas of weakness.

I particularly like sharing the story of the major league baseball pitcher, Jim Abbott. Born and raised in Flint, Michigan, Jim Abbott had only a stub of a right arm with little upper arm and no forearm. All he had was a small hand literally attached to his elbow. Fortunately for Jim, his parents did not want him to use that as an excuse and encouraged him to do whatever he wanted. He wanted to play baseball. So he taught himself to use a baseball glove, to pitch, and even to hit with a bat. He became good enough at switching his glove off his left hand quickly enough so that he could pitch. He was an outstanding pitcher with the University of Michigan's baseball team. After a short minor league experience, he made it to the big leagues, pitching for the California Angels and the New York Yankees. One year he even had a no-hitter—one of the hallmarks of an outstanding pitcher.

If a virtually one-armed player like Jim Abbott could make it to the big leagues, then what excuses do the rest of us have?

To be sure, all of us have self-defeating behaviors. Every one of us has quirks, foibles, health conditions, bad habits, emotional hang-ups, and whatever else keep us from working hard at or accomplishing a goal. It may help to share some of your own with your child, particularly if you've managed to overcome them.

I let the young people with whom I work know that I've had a few self-defeating behaviors in my time. Kids in my treatment groups are usually amazed when I tell them my shyness has held me back and played havoc with my anxiety level. "You're not shy!" teens say. Some have said, "I can't believe you were ever shy."

But the fact is I grew up thinking I was shy . . . and I acted that way. I always really wanted to be performing in front of others, but instead I felt very inadequate and became a shrinking violet. When I became a psychologist and I'd get invitations to speak in front of groups, I would break out in cold sweats and worry myself sick. As much as I wanted to do this, I was afraid of what others would think of me. I was fearful I wouldn't do a good job. This bothered me throughout most of my school life. I couldn't ask questions in class and felt terribly ill at ease getting up in front of other students to give reports or speeches.

But I knew there were things I wanted to do. I wanted to help people by giving speeches and workshops. I wanted to spread my message by going on radio and television. I wanted to write a column for newspapers. I also wanted to write books. I knew that I'd have to get over my fears to reach these goals.

So I tell teenagers who say they can't get over their self-defeating behaviors about my own fears and hang-ups and how they held me back for a long time. But I still made my goals, and then I went out of my way to do the things that made me afraid. I accepted every speech and speaking engagement that came along.

I went on radio and television—even when I wasn't interested in the show or in the publicity. And you can guess what happened. I got less shy and much more comfortable.

By the time my second book came out and I was finally booked on a national talk show where somewhere around 30 million people would see me, I wasn't all that nervous. Even my wife, my children and my best friends said I didn't look all that anxious. I had really gotten over the self-defeating part of my shyness.

Now I tell the adolescents with whom I work that if I can do that, then no matter what their self-defeating behavior is, they can overcome it.

"I DON'T HAVE ANY SELF-DEFEATING BEHAVIORS"

Some teenagers have fairly good self-esteem, even if they have many problems in their life or have much that they could—or should—change. But it is not uncommon for me to encounter teenagers who steadfastly maintain that they don't have any self-defeating behaviors. And some even really believe it.

I find that the best way to deal with this unawareness is to point out some of my own self-defeating behaviors, such as my shyness or sometimes being disorganized or having a problem with spelling, without taking steps to improve it. Another way to approach this is to point out some of the self-defeating behaviors of other teenagers I know. But just asking some pointed questions can help.

Recently a 14-year-old boy named Mike told me he didn't have any self-defeating behaviors. "Of course you do," I said in reply. "Everyone has some."

"Not me," Mike replied.

"Okay," I said. "Let me ask you this. How are you doing in school?"

"Okay," he said.

"But you could be doing better?" I suggested.

"Yeah, I could," Mike said.

"What keeps you from doing better?" I asked. "Are you not smart?"

"No, that's not it," Mike said.

"Okay, what is the reason?" I asked.

"Well, sometimes I don't bring my work home. I don't always get to it because I put it off. And I skip class sometimes."

"So you're saying that you sometimes skip, you don't do all your work, and you don't even always bring homework home to do. Right?" Mike nodded.

"Those sound like self-defeating behaviors to me," I continued, "because I think you'd like to get better grades. Right?" He said he did.

"Consider those some of your self-defeating behaviors for now," I said. It was difficult for him to argue much at that point that they weren't self-defeating behaviors.

That's not to say that teens will know how to deal with their self-defeating behaviors once they are identified. The most important thing is that they know they have some. Calling them self-defeating behaviors is a critical factor here. They are not called disorders or conditions or diagnoses or anything else that can get them off the hook. They are actions for which they are totally responsible and that they can change if they choose to.

WHAT ABOUT REAL DISORDERS?

What about when kids do have serious disorders or disabilities—things such as dyslexia, attention deficit hyperactivity disorder, serious learning disabilities, or a diagnosed depression? Yes, those are real problems, I admit. But adolescents can let problem areas or weaknesses be debilitating, or they can do something about them. We can use excuses, or we can try to overcome our handicaps and disabilities. Having only one functional arm would be a handicap if you wanted to be a baseball player. But that's all it is—a handicap, not an excuse or a license to quit.

That's the message we have to get across to teenagers: that they have no license to give up on themselves. I can't think of anyone who had more of a license to quit than Helen Keller, who lost her sight and her hearing at age two. Yet look at what she accomplished in her life. She wrote thirteen books and lectured widely on various causes. If we can get that message across to adolescents, we can encourage them to try—no matter what things get in the way. It is up to them to do something with both the gifts and the handicaps that life has handed them.

COMMON SELF-DEFEATING BEHAVIORS

I see many self-defeating behaviors in teenagers. Here's a list that came from some of the teens with whom I've worked recently:

Smoking
Not studying for school
Not learning how to take notes at school
Not being able to find a job
Getting kicked out of school
Using drugs
Having a bad temper
Being lazy
Giving up on himself or herself
Swearing
Hanging around with the wrong kids
Getting too mad too easily

Having a bad attitude at school
Not paying attention
Not obeying his or her parents

All of these self-defeating behaviors get in the way of kids accomplishing goals important to them.

Sixteen-year-old Leslie had been in conflict with her parents for several years. She wanted to live on her own and be independent. To try to attain this goal, she called the police on her parents, falsely reported that they beat her up, and lied about her age— among other things. She had no bruises, and her parents were co-operative with the police. The police did not arrest her parents, nor did they believe Leslie's report. In fact, they came close to prosecuting her for giving a false police report. If anything, Leslie was farther from achieving her real goal. Lying and making up stories to friends and the police were self-defeating behaviors for her because they interfered with her accomplishing her goal of becoming more independent.

After this crisis when I met with Leslie, I talked to her about her goal and about some of her self-defeating behaviors. "If you want to live independently," I told her, "you're going to have to eliminate some self-defeating behaviors. Lying, giving false police reports, and not working will not help you to get closer to your goal of living on your own. The chances are those behaviors will hold you back and make it longer before you get to where you want to be."

Leslie could understand that. "So what do I have to do?" she asked.

"Let's brainstorm that," I said, "and see how you can eliminate the self-defeating behaviors that stand in your way." Leslie was agreeable. As we talked about the ideas, it was Leslie who was now saying that she would have to make changes. It didn't have to come from me. I should point out that I didn't necessarily encourage her goal to be independent. But recognizing that I couldn't talk Leslie out of her goal to live away from her parents, the next best thing was to help her deal with her goal in a realistic way while trying to change her serious self-defeating behaviors. I thought that if she actually made changes in her behavior, she would get along better with her parents and might decide to delay moving out.

Leslie identified several self-defeating behaviors that interfered with reaching her goal to be independent. She realized that fighting with her parents strengthened their resolve to keep her at home. She also recognized that she needed them as allies rather than as enemies. By examining herself, her actual goals, and her self-defeating behaviors, she stopped blaming her parents, took responsibility for her actions, and planned realistically to move out at a later time and with the cooperation of her parents.

OVERCOMING SELF-DEFEATING BEHAVIORS

How do adolescents best work on overcoming their self-defeating behaviors? They have to set some goals for overcoming them—just as they did in Chapter 2 with other life goals. The four steps involved are like those for goal-setting:

1. Identify your self-defeating behaviors.

2. Brainstorm ways to overcome these self-defeating behaviors. Use the best ideas to design an action plan.

3. Take the first step.

4. Evaluate your efforts to overcome your self-defeating behaviors and your action plan periodically, and make changes when necessary.

After your teen identifies her biggest self-defeating behaviors and puts them in the context of roadblocks to achieving her goals, then she must brainstorm ideas for eliminating or at least keeping the self-defeating behaviors under control.

Too often, I find teenagers tend to be lazy thinkers (perhaps another self-defeating behavior?); that is, their ideas for dealing with self-defeating behaviors are superficial and likely to be far from effective. For example, when I asked Chad how he would work on his problem of not paying attention in school, he said, "I'll pay attention more." When examining their self-defeating behavior of not completing homework, other kids might say, "I'll start completing my homework."

Well, yes, those are things to do, but if it was so easy, why weren't they already doing this? The answer, of course, is that it's not that easy. In order to cope successfully with a self-defeating behavior, the adolescent will have to engage in some thinking to come up with an action plan. As the parent, your best role is to ask the tough questions. For the teen who said he'd start paying attention, the question is, "And how are you going to do that?" Keep asking that until your teen has come up with a workable action plan.

Suppose a teen's problem was being late for school. A workable action plan would sound something like this: "I'll overcome my problem of being late for school by setting my alarm clock for six o'clock in the morning. I'll also make sure I go to bed by ten o'clock at night so that I get enough sleep. Since I don't always hear the alarm, I'll ask my mother to make sure I'm up by ten minutes after six. I will eat breakfast and be dressed by seven o'clock and leave for the bus by ten after seven."

Every so often, there should be an evaluation to see how he's doing. Is he making headway with his self-defeating behaviors? Is he still making progress or has he given up? Does he need to revise or change the action plan? Review these questions with your adolescent.

GOLDEN OPPORTUNITIES TO TEACH ABOUT SELF-DEFEATING BEHAVIORS

As with every step in this book, there are golden opportunities to teach lessons about self-defeating behaviors.

One of the most accessible and easiest has to do with our own self-defeating behaviors. Because even we parents have them and because most of us are usually working on one or more at most times in our adult lives, sharing this with our teens can be useful and instructive.

Losing weight, stopping smoking, increasing the number of healthy habits, changing personal habits (like swearing too much), improving work habits (like working more efficiently), being a better parent (by expressing less anger or impatience or by having fewer overly high expectations, for instance), and decreasing stress levels are some typical goals many adults I know have as they try to overcome self-defeating behaviors.

Letting our teens know the self-defeating behaviors to which we have given priority and how we're trying to overcome them can be instructive for them. They can learn from us about selecting a self-defeating behavior and about how an adult works hard at changing one.

Besides modeling the right way to go about selecting and changing a self-defeating behavior, you can be available when your teen comes to you with a problem. If you have a good relationship, your child will share many problems as they arise.

WHEN YOUR TEEN SHARES A PROBLEM

Sometimes teens come to their parents in some of the following ways:

"Could I talk to you about my grades?"
"I wanted to warn you that you won't like my report card."
"I don't know why I can't get a date for the Spring Dance."
"Everyone picks on me."
"My math teacher doesn't like me."

These kinds of problems are common in the lives of teenagers, so if you pay attention, you're bound to find many golden opportunities to talk about self-defeating behaviors.

If there's one thing that causes consternation with parents and often leads to arguments between parents and their teens, it's grades at school. Yet, the reason why many adolescents aren't living up to their own or their parents' expectations has to do with the teens' own self-defeating behaviors.

You don't have to be heavy-handed about telling your child what she needs to do to overcome a self-defeating behavior, but keep the idea in mind when you begin discussing the reasons why her grades are slipping or why she's in danger of failing a class.

How can you best discuss grades and school performance with an eye on helping your child change self-defeating behaviors? I find the best way is focusing on the solution rather than concentrating on the problem. And while you're doing this, you want to put some—if not all—of the responsibility back on your teen. Questions like "What do you think is going wrong in biology so that your grades are dropping?" or "What's different this marking period in history?" help to focus on the reason for the problem and help to avoid a defensive reaction from your teen because you're not attacking her.

Help her examine the causes for the problem in an objective way by asking questions that are not critical. You can play a much more useful role if you simply ask probing questions rather than point out the answer or be the know-it-all.

When you've helped her find some of the reasons for the problem, the next step is to help her decide what can be changed. Often these will be her self-defeating behaviors. It's commonplace for parents to say, "You're going to have to study harder." Those kinds of trite and obvious comments and suggestions are virtually worthless and are, if anything, discouraging. Better that you ask, "What do you think, based on what you think the problem is, that you'll have to do to improve your biology grade?"

Try to get your adolescent to look at the roadblocks to his goals on his own and in a fairly objective way, to decide what he has to change, and then to take steps to work on those changes. Don't take over and do it for him. If your child feels excluded from a major role in the process, he is likely to make superficial agreements to change, based on pleasing you or ending a discussion.

SERIOUS PROBLEMS ARE GOLDEN OPPORTUNITIES, TOO

When a notice from a local court came to the home of Jeremy, age 16, his father opened it. It was a ticket indicating that Jeremy had been charged with driving while intoxicated. Jeremy's father was stunned. Jeremy had not told either parent of his arrest.

While situations like these are shockers for parents, they are also golden opportunities to help your child deal with self-defeating behaviors. If Jeremy wishes to keep his driver's license, to avoid going to jail or having his car impounded by the police, or to stay on track to go to college, he must avoid using alcohol when he's driving. Clearly such use is a self-defeating behavior.

How will his father best approach Jeremy to teach a lesson about dealing with the self-defeating behavior of drinking and driving? Drinking and driving is no longer considered a behavior that parents or teens can shrug off as just harmless teenage experimentation or a rite of initiation into adult life. Our society recognizes it as dangerous and illegal behavior that threatens the lives of other motorists and pedestrians. So you need to treat it seriously. Yet there is a lesson to be learned even about something that is a serious self-defeating behavior. If Jeremy drives after drinking again, he could kill someone, be imprisoned, or could be killed himself.

But how does a parent get this across and teach a teenager a lesson in the process? A conversation could go like this:

FATHER: "I saw in today's mail that you got a ticket for having alcohol in the car and being intoxicated while driving. I wish you had told me before I saw the ticket."

JEREMY: "Yeah, I know. I should have told you. I'm sorry."

FATHER: "So, what now?"

JEREMY: "What do you mean?"

FATHER: "Well, this is a pretty serious problem, not to mention that you shouldn't be drinking at all. What do you plan to do about it?"

JEREMY: "I'll pay for my tickets and do whatever the court tells me to do."

FATHER: "That's good. But there's a more serious issue here—your drinking and driving."

JEREMY: "Well, this was something I had never done before, and I will never do it again."

FATHER: "I hope not. But I'm concerned about *making sure* this doesn't happen again because the next time it could be fatal for you, your passengers, or other innocent people. There can be no slipups in your assurance to never drink and drive again. I wonder how you can make sure this won't happen again."

JEREMY: "I just won't drink anymore."

FATHER: "But I know this isn't the first time you've had alcohol. I'm not easily convinced that you'll never drink and drive again. So tell me how you can stop drinking."

JEREMY: "I just won't drink anymore."

FATHER: "I know right now sitting here that that's what you mean. I think at this moment that you believe you never will. But I know that no matter how sound your intentions right now, you might be tempted when you go to a party or you're around friends who drink."

JEREMY: "I know. I guess I'll just try to stay away from kids who are drinking."

FATHER: "What else could you do?"

JEREMY: "I could tell my friends I can't ever drink and drive again. I could call you if I've been drinking and have you come and pick me up. I could make it a rule to never have more than one drink."

FATHER: "Those sound more realistic. Why don't you write them down so neither one of us will forget them and then we can talk more about how you're doing with these ideas. Okay?"

JEREMY: "Sure."

The drinking and driving were identified by Jeremy's father as a self-defeating behavior although he never used those words with his son. Nonetheless, he handled the situation in such a way that Jeremy finally came up with a plan for dealing with this particular self-defeating behavior problem.

Jeremy's father took advantage of a serious situation to help teach Jeremy how to handle a major self-defeating behavior. Whether your adolescent presents you with a major self-defeating behavior such as this one or with less serious ones, how this father dealt with it is a model for you to follow in asking the right questions, maintaining a serious tone, and helping to guide the discussion toward a concrete plan of action to help decrease a self-defeating behavior.

PUTTING IT INTO ACTION

Use this worksheet with your teen either by having him or her fill it out or by reading it aloud and filling it out together.

SELF-DEFEATING BEHAVIORS WORKSHEET

A. *Identify Your Self-Defeating Behaviors:*

1. What things are likely to get in your way of accomplishing your most important goals? List those things below:

   a.

   b.

   c.

   d.

   e.

   f.

   g.

2. Choose the one or two most serious self-defeating behaviors and write them here:

   a.

   b.

B. *Brainstorm ways to overcome these self-defeating behaviors. Use the best ideas to design an action plan.*

1. Write down as many ideas as you can to overcome your first self-defeating behavior:

   a.

   b.

   c.

      d.

      e.

2. Write down as many ideas as you can to overcome your second self-defeating behavior:

      a.

      b.

      c.

      d.

      e.

C. *Take the First Step:*

For each of your self-defeating behaviors, write down your plan of action and the first step you will take, beginning tomorrow:

1. My plan of action to overcome my first self-defeating behavior:

    a. My plan of action will be to do the following things:

        (1)

        (2)

        (3)

        (4)

        (5)

    b. The first step I will take tomorrow to begin to overcome this self-defeating behavior is: _____ .

    c. Other things I will do this week to begin working at this are:

        (1)

        (2)

        (3)

    d. I plan to overcome this self-defeating behavior by this date:_____ .

2. My plan of action to overcome my second self-defeating behavior:

    a. My plan of action will be to do the following things:

        (1)

        (2)

        (3)

        (4)

        (5)

    b. The first step I will take tomorrow to begin to overcome this self-defeating behavior is: _____ .

    c. Other things I will do this week to begin working at this are:

        (1)

        (2)

        (3)

    d. I plan to overcome this self-defeating behavior by this date:_____ .

4

STEP THREE: TEACH YOUR TEENAGER TO BE ASSERTIVE

Y ou have to be aggressive to be the top-selling salesperson in your company or your industry. In today's business world many say you have to be aggressive just to get ahead at all.

Our children have to be aggressive in order to survive in an aggressive world. In order to deal with the bullies they'll inevitably encounter in school and on the playground, many parents believe that children should be taught to box or to use a form of martial arts.

Our culture reveres strength, power, and aggressive winning. The sagas of the Old West had this theme, and it has continued in Hollywood with film after film dedicated to the proposition that a hero with a quick gun or a powerful fist can save the day.

Yet one of the leading causes of death for teenagers in our country is violence. Adolescents who are aggressive appear more likely to become a statistic—by dying young or by entering the judicial system. At best, aggressive teenagers have considerably more difficulty winning and keeping friends.

At the heart of the conventional wisdom, I believe, is confusion. Adolescents and their parents are confused about what it means to be aggressive versus what it means to be assertive, probably because many people consistently use the two words—*aggressive* and *assertive*—interchangeably. Little wonder that our children and teens are confused about the proper way to act in many situations.

WHAT IT MEANS TO BE ASSERTIVE

There are three possible ways of reacting in most situations: being passive, being aggressive, or being assertive.

The *passive* person makes excuses, cannot express herself openly or honestly, and is more likely to give in rather than to stand up for what she thinks is right.

The *aggressive* person, on the other hand, reacts with hostility and will attack when threatened or in a conflict. He will try to resolve problems by hurting others or by threatening violence. The only way to stand up for himself, he believes, is to be on the attack. A *passive-aggressive* person takes a passive approach with aggressive, hostile intentions.

The *assertive* person acts differently than either the passive or the aggressive ones. She knows how to express what she wants and what she needs. She can express herself openly and honestly. She knows how to be her best self. She shows self-confidence when she needs to be herself. She can confidently say no to someone else when she has to. And she can stand up for what she believes is right.

While there are times in life to be either passive or aggressive, it is my belief that learning how to be assertive can lead to much better and more successful interpersonal relationships. At the same time, assertiveness can help teenagers avoid fights and the kind of violence that has become common among children and teens and that frequently results in legal and social trouble for juveniles.

There's plenty of evidence and statistics that show that violent and aggressive problem solving is ineffective and unsuccessful. We can teach our teens a better way.

Many years ago two teenage boys I knew got into an argument. As so often happens, one thing led to another and they squared off in a field near their high school to fight it out. The first boy took a swing and hit the other in the jaw, knocking him down. When the boy fell, his head hit a small rock and he died instantly. The boy who had taken one swing was charged with murder, convicted of manslaughter, and was sentenced to prison as an adult.

A tragic story? Yes. But it was one of those stories that wouldn't have been remembered more than two days if it had the usual outcome when boys get together and try to resolve differences with their fists. It was just boys being boys. That's all it was supposed to be. But an unpredictable circumstance changed everything. I've always thought it so sad that these two boys didn't know how to be assertive and resolve differences in a more effective way. One boy would be alive, and the other would be leading a normal life outside of prison walls.

TEACHING ASSERTIVENESS

What are the most important aspects of teaching assertiveness to your teenager? I believe there are two aspects to consider. The first is teaching them the difference between assertiveness and aggression, which is sometimes a very subtle point to adolescents. The second is to convince them that assertiveness can have a role in their lives and that it won't compromise their integrity, manhood, or womanhood.

I begin teaching the difference between assertiveness and aggressiveness by challenging adolescents to find examples in movies or in real life of people solving problems in an assertive or an aggressive way. "Bring me in examples," I say to them. "Let's see if you can tell the difference."

And what do they bring in as examples? Usually, it's a scene from a recent movie. If it stars Arnold Schwarzenegger or Sylvester Stallone, they don't have to show me or describe it. I know it's aggressive and not assertive. If it's an incident from real life, they will tell a story about some incident they witnessed. They will claim it was not aggressive because no one was hit or beat up. However, more times than not, there was a threat.

And therein lies the problem for many of the teens I know. They have grown up by watching so much violence on TV, in the movies, in school, and in their own homes that they are relatively immune to violence. What seems violent to me tends to be relatively benign to them. In their world, an aggressive threat isn't all that violent. It's only violent when someone is killed. Shooting someone with a handgun, most will admit, is aggressive.

The task we have before us with adolescents is to sensitize them to violence and aggression in their many forms. Rarely if ever does a teen come in with a legitimate example of a friend or movie character acting in an assertive manner. So, if they can't recognize assertive behavior, they have to be taught what it is, even if it means spoonfeeding.

With the teens, I immediately point out any of their words or actions that are aggressive. I also let them know when someone is assertive. I want them to begin to ask themselves in many kinds of situations, "Was that assertive or aggressive?"

Then we do an exercise. It's called "What Would You Say Next?"

In the exercise, I give them six situations. I ask them to look them over and to decide what they would say next in order to give an assertive—not aggressive—response. Try these with your own teen.

1. Your friend is mad because someone beat up a friend of yours and his. He says to you: "Let's go kick his ass! Let's show him he can't get away with beating up our friend!"

You do not think this is the best way to handle the situation, and you say: _____

2. Your mother wants you to take the classes she thinks are important for you. She says: "You should take more algebra next year. The more math you take the better for you."

You are not interested in making math your major, and you say: _____

3. Your gym teacher says to you: "You'd be great on the volleyball team. Why don't you sign up and come out to practice next Tuesday. Remember, I'm counting on you!"

You're not interested in volleyball, and you say: _____

4. The police officer is sure you helped steal a car and says: "Why don't you come clean and tell me you took the car. I'll see that things go easy for you if you tell me the truth, and we can get this cleared up. Okay?"

You didn't steal the car, and you say: _____

5. You handed in a homework assignment, but the teacher says: "I can't find that report you said you turned in. Sorry, but I guess you'll just have to do it over again tonight and hand it in tomorrow."

You say: _____

6. You're trying to cut down on smoking marijuana, but your friend, who just bought some marijuana, says: "Why don't you come over this afternoon after school. We'll just hang out, listen to some music, and smoke a little. Okay?"

You say: _____

Then we go around the group, and I ask everyone to try their hand at one of these. When their responses are either aggressive or passive, I let them know immediately. Then we work on responses until there is an assertive one for each example that sounds like something a contemporary teen would say.

These examples become important because they are similar to some of the real-life situations that teens often encounter. If they can learn assertive ways to handle these situations, they may be able to remember to say something similar in like situations when they actually occur for them.

"But no one really would handle it that way," they often tell me. Or they'll retort, "That's wimpy," as I try to teach them about assertiveness.

If your child says something like that, point out that it takes courage and strength to hold back anger and to speak up to someone in a forceful way. The hardest part is saying what you really feel.

To give you a better idea of how passive, aggressive, and assertive responses differ, I'll give examples of responses adolescents have used in the six situations.

1. Your friend is mad because someone beat up a friend of yours and his. He says to you: "Let's go kick his ass! Let's show him he can't get away with beating up our friend!"

You do not think this is the best way to handle the situation, and you say:

A *passive* response: "If you want to, I'll go with you."

An *aggressive* response: "Yeah, let's go beat him up. I hate his guts."

An *assertive* response: "I think there's a better way to handle this. I'm not fighting."

2. Your mother wants you to take the classes she thinks are important for you. She says: "You should take more algebra next year. The more math you take the better for you."

You are not interested in making math your major, and you say:

A *passive* response: "Okay, if you say so."

An *aggressive* response: "I'm not going to take more math. Stay out of my business!"

An *assertive* response: "I understand that you think it's in my best interest to take more math classes. But I really struggle with math, and I know it will make next year more difficult for me. I feel strongly that I'd be better off taking a science class."

3. Your gym teacher says to you: "You'd be great on the volleyball team. Why don't you sign up and come out to practice next Tuesday. Remember, I'm counting on you!"

You're not interested in volleyball, and you say:

A *passive* response: "Sure, Coach, I'll probably come by tomorrow."

An *aggressive* response: "I hate volleyball. I think it's really a dumb sport, so forget it!"

An *assertive* response: "Thanks, but it's not a sport I'm interested in right now. I really appreciate your asking me, and if I change my mind I'll let you know."

4. The police officer is sure you helped steal a car and says: "Why don't you come clean and tell me you took the car. I'll see that things go easy for you if you tell me the truth, and we can get this cleared up. Okay?"

You didn't steal the car, and you say:

A *passive* response: "I don't know why everyone picks on me. I didn't do nothing, and I don't know nothing."

An *aggressive* response: "You cops are all the same! I'm not going to help you at all. If you think I did something, charge me!"

An *assertive* response: "I am telling you the truth. I had nothing to do with this crime. But if I hear anything about it in the neighborhood, I'll call you."

5. You handed in a homework assignment, but the teacher says: "I can't find that report you said you turned in. Sorry, but I guess you'll just have to do it over again tonight and hand it in tomorrow."

You say:

A *passive* response: "Well, if you can't find it, I guess I'll just do it over."

An *aggressive* response: "You lost it, that's your problem. I'm not doing it over!"

An *assertive* response: "I understand that homework gets lost sometimes, but I worked really hard on that assignment. What about me helping you try to find it. If we can't find it, let's see what we can work out about this situation. Okay?"

6. You're trying to cut down on smoking marijuana, but your friend, who just bought some marijuana, says: "Why don't you come over this afternoon after school. We'll just hang out, listen to some music, and smoke a little. Okay?"

You say:

A *passive* response: "This afternoon? Okay."

An *aggressive* response: "Don't you know I'm trying to stop? You better stay away from me or I'll beat the crap out of you."

An *assertive* response: "No thanks, I'm trying to stop smoking weed. I'd appreciate it if you didn't ask me again."

EVERYONE HAS BASIC RIGHTS

Aggressive responses violate the rights of others. That's why it's important that you teach your adolescent the rights that he and other people have. When he knows these rights, he will be in a far better position to decide when his responses or behavior are passive, aggressive, or assertive.

The four rights that we all share are:

1. You have the right to act in your own best interest.
2. You have the right to ask for things, and you have the right to refuse what others are asking for.
3. You have the right to not be bullied or intimidated.
4. You have the right to make a mistake and change your mind.

Acting in Your Own Best Interest

Every individual has the right to decide what is best for her and to be her own best self. This means that if someone is trying to convince you to go against what you want to do or what you think is best for you, they are acting aggressively. The more they persist in trying to convince you or to pressure you, the more aggressive their behavior. By being aggressive, they are interfering with one of your personal rights.

To be assertive, a teen will often have to make decisions about what is best for him. Terry, a 16-year-old boy who is on probation to the juvenile court for stealing, wants very much to get off probation. When a friend applied pressure to Terry to try to convince him to go out drinking one Saturday night, Terry responded in an assertive manner. "Look, you go out and get drunk if you want to. But leave me out. I want to get off probation soon and I can't do that by drinking."

His friend persisted by saying, "What's the harm? You won't get caught and nothing can go wrong."

"That's easy for you to say," Terry said. "But I thought that before and look where it got me. So the answer is no. I'm going home and staying there tonight. Goodbye."

Terry acted in his own best interest. As his friend pressured him, this friend was becoming aggressive. Terry stood up to him by being honest and straightforward. He didn't get angry and he didn't threaten him. But he stuck to what was best for him.

Asking for What You Want/Refusing a Request

Adolescents need to know that there is no harm in asking for something, and in fact in many instances they have a right to make a request for something they want. Teens need to be taught that they are acting within their rights by requesting money from a parent, asking someone out on a date, requesting an extension on a class report, or asking for time off from work.

But they also need to know that everyone also has an equal right to refuse or to turn down a request. As a parent, you can refuse to give your child the money she's requested. Anyone can turn down a date. A teacher can refuse to give an extension on a report. And the manager at work can say no when an employee wants to take a night off.

Of course, we would all like to have our requests accepted. But pressuring, getting mad, or even threatening the person who has denied a request becomes aggressive. That can work both ways, too.

When Janie asked her mother if six friends could come over on Saturday night to watch videos and have pizza, her mother said no. Janie forgot that her mother had every right to deny this kind of request. It turned out her mother had good reasons for saying no—Janie had waited until the last minute to ask; and the last time she had friends over, one of those friends sneaked beer in the house, which they drank. But even if she didn't have good reasons for saying no, she still had the right to say no. When Janie got angry and berated her mother for turning this request down, she was forgetting *her mother's* rights, and she was acting in an aggressive way.

Because Janie and her mother had been discussing aggressive and assertive behavior, her mother pointed out that Janie had crossed the line into aggressiveness. Janie had to agree and she apologized.

Our teens also have the right to say no, and others should respect that right. When 15-year-old Richard was invited to a party where he knew there would be alcohol and drugs, he said no. His friend Lisa really put the pressure on him. Richard said no several times, but Lisa kept trying to convince him that if he didn't go he would miss out on the fun and that he was being disloyal to her by refusing. Lisa was aggressive in this instance. In effect, when it is forgotten that a person has the right to reject a request, that person's right is being violated. What teens have to learn and re-member is that aggression occurs when an individual's rights are trampled on.

Resisting Bullying and Intimidation

If you allow yourself to be bullied or intimidated into going along with what someone else wants, they are being aggressive, but you are acting in a passive way.

Consider this situation in Alishia's house. When Alishia's mother says she can't go out at night with her friends, Alishia engages in bullying tactics with her mother.

"Why can't I go?" Alishia starts out. "It's early, and I won't come in late."

As her mother tries to hold her ground, Alishia applies more and more pressure. "Everyone else gets to go out on school nights," she says, as her voice gets louder and more insistent. "I'm not going to get in any trouble. You know that. I don't know why you don't trust me."

No matter what her mother says in response, it's not satisfactory to Alishia, who only wants her mother to cave in and let her go out. When this response is not forthcoming, Alishia hauls out the heavy guns of intimidation. "If you don't let me go, I'll hate you," she says angrily. "I'll run away and you'll never see me again. What's the use of living here, you never let me do anything. I hate *you!*"

Alishia's aggressiveness violates her mother's right not to be bullied or intimidated. But because she's used this tactic in the past and it has worked on occasion, she doesn't care about her mother's rights. Alishia wants what she wants.

But if the shoe were on the other foot, if Alishia were being pressured by her mother or someone else, she would feel the unfairness and the threat that accompanies such bullying.

In fact, Alishia has experienced this. Even though she's only 14 years old, she has been in situations with older boys where she has been pressured into a sexual relationship. She hates feeling coerced into having sex, and she can certainly agree that this isn't fair to her. What she has difficulty understanding is that both she and her mother have rights in regard to being pressured into something they don't want to do.

Alishia's mother calmly told Alishia that her response was aggressive and therefore not acceptable. Alishia was not happy, but she realized that her response had been inappropriate.

Making Mistakes/Changing Your Mind

Teens need to understand that they have the right to make mistakes. No one is perfect, and all of us at times use poor judgment. Sometimes we put ourselves in situations where we shouldn't be. At times teens agree to something that later they think was stupid. But by then, they often think, it's too late to back out.

not so. Adolescents don't have to be that hard on themselves—or on others. Everyone is entitled to mistakes of judgment. And when they've made miscalculations and used poor judgment, they can often correct the mistake. This is because they have the right to change their mind.

If Alex agrees to skip school the last hour, he has a chance to think about it. After giving it some thought, he might conclude it was dumb to agree to skip the last hour when he hasn't been in any trouble so far this semester. But he promised his best friend he would skip. Doesn't he have to keep his promise?

No. Alex can remember that he has the right to make mistakes, and he has the right to change his mind and correct an error. When his friend meets him at the end of his sixth-hour class and says, "Let's go before anyone sees us," Alex can tell him he's changed his mind. Alex can say: "Look, I've changed my mind. I've been thinking about it and decided it's not a good idea to skip. So I'm going to seventh hour."

What if his friend pressures him? Then Alex has to recall all of his rights. He has the right to act in his own best interest, and he has the right to not be bullied or pressured. If his friend puts pressure on him, Alex can be assertive: "I feel like you're pressuring me to do something I don't want to do," Alex can say. "If you're really my friend, you'll understand that I changed my mind. If you want to skip seventh hour, that's up to you. But I'm not going to. And I don't want you to pressure me anymore."

THE ASSERTIVE SKILLS TEENS
NEED TO LEARN

There are several essential skills that make up assertiveness.

- *Choosing the right words.* In being assertive, the right

words are those that allow you to be honest and direct while expressing how you feel.

For instance, if an adolescent is being pressured to do something she doesn't want to do, such as riding in a car with a driver who is intoxicated, she can be honest and direct by saying exactly how she feels: "I feel very unsafe riding with you after you've been drinking. I'm going to find another way to get home."

If she continues to get pressure, she can say how she feels about the pressure: "I feel like you're trying to force me to do something I have said I don't want to do."

Then she can state clearly what she wants: "I want you to stop pressuring me because my mind is made up. I'm going to find someone else to take me home."

• *Eye contact.* This is vital because the other person has to know that you're serious. When you move closer to the other person, look them in the eye, and hold that eye contact, the other person will get the message that you are saying something important.

• *Body language.* Body language is the nonverbal way you get across your point to another person without uttering a word. By standing up straight and tall and having a serious look on your face, you indicate without equivocation that you're saying something they should listen to. If you're looking at the ground, slouching, and grinning, there's little chance the other person is going to take you seriously.

• *Voice quality.* This says a lot about your message. A wimpy, pleading, or whining voice isn't going to convince anyone to stop trying to intimidate you or to desist from teasing you. But, when you project a strong, firm, no-nonsense voice, along with serious body language, eye contact, and the right words, there is a very good chance that you are going to be absolutely convincing.

MORE TECHNIQUES TO MAKE
ASSERTIVENESS WORK

As you're teaching your teenager about assertiveness, you must pass on some of the techniques that will come in handy in different situations.

I've already mentioned that expressing your own needs and feelings is important so that you show your child how to do it. By expressing how he feels, your adolescent is more likely to be successful in his attempt at assertiveness.

In the following conversation Justin lets his girlfriend Nancy know how he feels. "Nancy, there's something that's been bothering me and I think we should talk about it," Justin said one day.

"Okay, Justin, what's up?" Nancy asked.

"It's about Ray," said Justin. "You hang around with him too much."

"Wait a minute!" said Nancy starting to sound angry. "Ray and I have been friends for a long time. You know I'm not interested in him as a boyfriend."

"I know that's what you tell me," said Justin, "but I get worried when you spend so much time with another boy. And besides that, I kinda feel left out at times."

Justin is very direct and honest in this beginning to the conversation. He lets Nancy know what's bothering him and how it makes him feel.

Furthermore, Justin has avoided attacking Nancy. If he had made accusations right off the bat, the conversation would very likely have become an argument. Because Justin was not aggressive, the discussion has to move on to how he feels. If they had started arguing, Justin may never have accomplished his real purpose, which was to discuss his feelings.

As the conversation continues, though, Nancy brings up some irrelevant issues.

"You're just trying to make me give up all my friends," Nancy said. "I don't like people trying to tell me what to do."

Justin had not asked her to give up any friends, nor did he tell her to do anything—at least not yet. She is trying to move the discussion into an argument, but Justin won't allow this to happen.

"I know that you just regard him as a friend and you're not really interested in him as a boyfriend," Justin said. "But you know I still worry about it."

In any assertive discussion, it's important to make a request, try to find some common ground for an agreement, or seek a compromise. Let's see how Justin and Nancy do.

"Yeah, so?" Nancy said defensively.

"Well, the problem is that even though I know you like Ray and don't want to give him up," Justin said, "I still feel funny about you hanging out with him, and I don't feel good about it when I know you're with him sometimes when you're not with me."

"I don't know why you're always yelling at me about this," said Nancy, who was getting irritated.

"Hold on a minute. Please let me finish," said Justin calmly, but firmly.

"Okay," replied Nancy.

"What I want to say is maybe we can try to solve this," Justin said.

"There's nothing to solve," replied Nancy, "except for you to be less possessive and jealous."

"Maybe so, but I think there is something to solve," said Justin.

"What?" asked Nancy.

"I think we can keep talking about this and maybe we can find a way for me to feel better about it," replied Justin.

"Like how?" Nancy asked.

"I told you how I felt," offered Justin, "maybe you could tell me how you feel about it."

"You already know how I feel."

"Not really," said Justin. "All I know is that you don't want to give up having Ray as your friend. What do you feel about what I said?"

"I feel like you're trying to control me and that you don't trust me."

"I think it would help if we knew where we stood with each other in this relationship," Justin said, not put off by her remark.

"I thought we knew," said Nancy. "You're my boyfriend!"

"I know," said Justin, "but sometimes I wonder if you might be interested in other guys or if you might go out on me."

"No, silly! I wouldn't do that. I like you a lot."

"Would you tell me if you wanted to stop going out with me or if there was someone you liked better?" Justin asked.

"Yes, I would," Nancy said.

"You wouldn't go out on me?"

"I promise. I wouldn't do that to someone."

"I feel the same way. I wouldn't go out on you either."

"Maybe there's something else we can agree to," said Nancy.

"What's that?"

"That you'll always talk to me and let me know when I do something that makes you angry or upset?"

"Even if it has to do with Ray?"

"Yes, even if it has to do with Ray. I know that my friendship with him upsets you, but as long as we can talk about it then we can always work out our problems. So, if it's Ray, please tell me. Okay?"

"I promise . . . as long as you don't get mad at me when I tell you how I feel."

"That's a deal."

The repeating technique is a very useful one when taking an assertive position. The same point is repeated until the other person hears it or accepts it.

This can work well when a teenager is resisting an attempt to be pressured into doing something he doesn't want to do. Whether it's a friend's attempt to persuade him to skip school, smoke marijuana, try crack, use steroids, ride in a car with a driver who's been drinking, or participate in doing something else that makes him feel uncomfortable, the idea with the broken-record technique is to take a position and stick to it.

When Barbara told her boyfriend she was not ready to have sex, he began to put pressure on her. At first it was mild, but over a period of weeks, the pressure was increased.

"Can't we do it?" Mike, her boyfriend, asked one night when they were watching a movie at his house.

"No, Mike," she said, "we can't."

"But why not?" he persisted.

"Because I'm not ready to have that kind of relationship," Barbara said, "so the answer is no."

"Please," Mike pleaded. "It would be okay. Really."

"No, Mike," she said, "the answer is no."

"Give me a good reason," he demanded.

"No," she said.

In this example, Barbara used the repeating technique by constantly saying "No." She didn't try to justify it, qualify it, or give reasons for it. She simply repeated it. And she was willing to do that until he understood that the answer would remain no.

Another assertive technique is to take command of the situation, tell the person pressuring you how you feel, and end the conversation.

In this situation between Mike and Barbara, if Mike kept pressuring her and continued to try to coerce her into having sex, she could use this technique. She would do so in the following way.

"Mike, I told you no," Barbara could say. "I've said no several times and my answer is not going to change. I don't like the way you're making me feel uncomfortable. If you keep pressuring me, I'm going to leave."

If Mike said anything further in an attempt to apply more pressure, Barbara could say, "I've asked you not to keep asking me. I'm sorry, but I'm leaving. Goodbye." At that point, she should turn on her heels and leave.

GOLDEN OPPORTUNITIES TO TEACH ASSERTIVENESS

Once you start looking, you'll find many opportunities to model assertiveness. The possibilities, in fact, are endless.

And I find that even in leading therapy groups with delinquents, I have many wonderful (and some not-so-wonderful opportunities) to show assertiveness in action.

Once in one of my groups we were meeting on Tuesday nights in a building in which the maintenance crew was cleaning when we met. There was a janitor who would vacuum right outside our door in the middle of our meeting every week. The kids and I found it disturbing.

One of the outspoken teenagers in the group said, "You're trying to teach us this assertiveness stuff, so why aren't you using it with him?"

I couldn't avoid that one. "You're right," I said. "I will handle this. Do you want to come with me?"

After group, this boy and I went to see the janitor. I said, "You know when you vacuum right outside our door, I have trouble talking over the sound of the vacuum. Can you please wait until our meeting is over to vacuum by our room?"

The man looked at both of us, hesitated, and then thought better about what he was probably thinking of saying and agreed. This boy could hardly wait until the next week to tell the rest of the group how "we" solved the problem by being assertive.

You'll find you can demonstrate assertiveness to your teenager when dealing with family members, neighbors, store clerks, telemarketers (especially those who call during dinner time soliciting for long-distance phone companies), teachers, and the teens themselves.

Disputes with neighbors are situations in which you'll have golden opportunities to handle problems in assertive ways while avoiding aggression. For instance, when a neighbor's tree is hanging over your property causing a problem with a power line, you have to speak with the neighbor. Being straightforward and making a request can settle the problem. Taking a more aggressive or threatening approach might start a feud that makes life miserable for both families. Saying nothing will cause you to feel resentful.

Something as simple as sending back a meal in a restaurant when that meal is not properly prepared or is cold is an excellent way of modeling assertiveness for a teenager. Taking back an item to a store after discovering that you bought the wrong one or that it's defective can also be a way of taking advantage of an opportunity to teach assertiveness.

Certainly, how you deal with family relationships and conflicts gives you many opportunities to talk about issues and problems in assertive ways. When 17-year-old Mel came home late several times when out with her friends, her mother approached her about the problem.

"We've got a problem we need to talk about," her mother said to her. "I thought we agreed that you'd be home by midnight on the weekends," her mother continued, "but your coming home late disrupts my sleep and sets a bad example for your brother. It also makes me think that your excuses about being late are ways of telling me that you're not going to honor our agreement."

"I don't know why you're yelling at me," Mel said becoming defensive and angry.

"I'm not yelling," her mother replied, "but we need to talk

about what's going on with our agreement. Do we have an agreement or not?"

No matter what Mel said from that point to shift the discussion or to focus on other issues (such as her mother's "yelling"), her mother stuck to the topic and persistently kept the conversation on track. By doing this, they avoided an argument and forged a new agreement that worked for both of them.

In the Robinson household, the children got to see their parents handle a husband-wife conflict in an assertive manner. It all started when Jim Robinson indicated he was planning to play golf on Saturday afternoon.

"Wait a minute!" his wife, Linda, said. "I thought you were going to help me get our house ready to put up for sale."

"I'll get to that next weekend," Jim said. "We've got plenty of time before we put this house on the market."

"No, we don't," countered Linda. "We've only got three weeks. Remember we agreed with the real estate agent. And we both said that there are several things that you need to do to enhance the value of this house."

"Are you saying I never help out around here?" Jim asked sounding irritated. The three Robinson children were watching this scene with intense interest.

"I'm not accusing you of anything," Linda replied, "but I expect you to put off more fun activities until we take care of the things that are necessary. I need help because I can't do this all by myself."

"I'll help you, Mommy," said 6-year-old Seth, who was sitting at the counter in the kitchen.

"No, darling," Linda said. "This is for your father and me to handle. I appreciate your offer, but daddy and I have to figure this out."

Looking at Jim, Linda asked, "So, what's it going to be—golf or work on this house?"

"I've been working hard at the office," he said, "but I also see your point. Maybe if we work real hard and get it done, I could still play golf later Sunday afternoon. What do you think?"

"That's possible," said Linda. "But thanks for compromising. Let's plan how we're going to tackle this work most efficiently this weekend."

"Okay," said Jim. "You guys want to help?" he said winking at the children.

PUTTING IT INTO ACTION

Plan projects for your teen that will teach her the differences between assertive, passive, and aggressive approaches to situations. Choose one or more of the following possible three projects or activities that you think will work best with your teen:

1. Ask him to think of a TV or movie character who shows passive, aggressive, and assertive responses in one or more scenes.

2. Arrange a role-play using one or more of the following situations:

- A friend wants her to do something she doesn't want to do.

- A parent wants her to take a course at school that doesn't interest her.

- A teacher is trying to persuade him to join the wrestling team, but he doesn't want to.

- A police officer is trying to get him to say he did something he didn't do.

- A kid at school is trying to get him to fight and he doesn't want to.

- The coach wants her to apologize for a mistake during a game, but she is sure she didn't make a mistake.
- A teacher says she didn't hand in her homework, but she's sure she did.
- Her friend wants her to sneak out at night, but she doesn't want to get in trouble.
- He's trying to stop drinking booze, but a friend wants him to come over and drink with him.
- A girl at school is spreading rumors about him and he wants it to stop.

3. Request that she take a situation in which she's currently involved and write her own short assertive role-play or script. The following points can give your teen direction:

- What will the role-play be about?
- Who will be the characters in it?
- Often to begin an assertive role-play, the first character says something that is meant to start an argument or fight. You then need to decide *who says what to whom.*
- Then, your main character (or the hero) in your role-play will *display assertive behavior.*
- Decide what the other person might do to make it difficult for the hero to be assertive. Your hero *sticks to being assertive.*
- Finish up with the hero *avoiding a fight or argument* by continuing to use assertive techniques.

5

STEP FOUR: TEACH YOUR TEENAGER TO HAVE FEELINGS FOR OTHERS

Paul, a 14-year-old boy, was riding in the car with his mother. On their way to a restaurant to have dinner together, Paul was clearly in a bad mood. When his mother asked him about school, he shot back at her, "What do you care?"

He continued to act in a rude and uncaring manner. Finally, after several sarcastic and unkind remarks to her, she pulled the car over to the side of the road to talk to Paul.

"Paul, I don't like it when you treat me so badly," she said emotionally. "I did nothing to you, and I expect you to treat me as politely as I treat you. Either you can speak to me in a respectful way, or you can get out of this car and walk."

Paul, angrily, opened the car door and jumped out. Because they were only a short way from the restaurant, his mother drove to the restaurant. She waited for him in the parking lot, and they entered the restaurant together, even though they weren't speaking. They didn't say anything to each other until the waitress took their order.

"I don't know why you made me mad and then made me walk," Paul said. "I didn't do anything to you. I just wanted to be left alone."

"I don't like it when you treat me that way, Paul," his mother said. "It hurts my feelings, and I'm sure it would hurt anyone you talked to in that same way."

"I don't know what you're talking about," Paul replied. And indeed it seemed that he didn't understand why his mother would be upset with him.

Most parents want to raise good children. Good kids, most of us parents would probably agree, are kind, generous, compassionate, and helpful to others.

When I asked some teenagers I know to guess the feelings of the parents of two teens killed in a recent school shooting by another adolescent, I got different answers.

Donald, age 14, said he thought the parents of the murdered teens would feel angry and confused. "They might feel confused because schools used to be considered safe, and now they aren't," Donald said.

On the other hand, Marcie, a 15-year-old girl, shrugged and said, "How should I know—I don't even follow the news."

HAVING EMPATHY

The difference between Donald and Marcie is striking. Marcie is an adolescent who gets into frequent fights, steals from her brother without feeling guilty, and seldom acts in kind, helpful, and compassionate ways toward others. She is not an empathetic, or empathic, individual—she is not able to understand the feelings of others.

Donald, on the other hand is an empathic teenager. He shows considerable feelings for others, cares what happens to people, and is capable—as indicated by his comment—of looking at situations from the point of view of another person.

Is having empathy for others all that important? You bet it is. When teenagers lack feelings for others and have little ability to see things from another's point of view, they have no built in sense of caring that causes them to avoid mistreating or hurting other people. In fact, I would say that most assaultive and violent teenagers have little ability to be empathic.

Researchers who have investigated empathy say that those individuals who are kind, compassionate, and caring generally do much better in a variety of interpersonal relationships. With these empathic characteristics teenagers will get along better in the family, at work, and in school. And there's a much better chance that stress in interpersonal relationships will be resolved in nonviolent ways.

The root of caring comes from the capacity for empathy. However, to be able to know what another individual feels, one has to be aware of one's own feelings. Daniel Goleman, in his book *Emotional Intelligence*, wrote that if people have no idea what they feel themselves, then they have no way of telling what someone else is feeling.

In some research, empathy has been found to be an inhibitor of aggressive behavior. For parents, this means that if you wish to protect your child or teen from becoming aggressive or violent, you must teach her or him as much empathy as you can.

Empathy develops gradually as young children grow. But some studies have shown that certain children are capable of showing distress and offering to help as early as ages one, two, or three.

Some children are born with the kind of temperament that allows them to show great concern when others are upset or distressed. But then there are other youngsters who come into this world with a temperament that predisposes them to be less concerned about the feelings of other people.

CAN EMPATHY BE TAUGHT?

For the most part, this question has been sidestepped in psychological studies. Yet, it is the basis of much psychotherapy and considerable work in institutions and in therapy programs designed for juvenile offenders and for those youngsters who have been neglected or abused.

However, we know from psychologists who have studied empathy in young people that those parents who are most caring and who have taught their children to be caring are most likely to have more caring and empathic children. When children have the opportunity to watch the actions of an empathic parent and when they love that parent and wish to emulate him or her, children learn to show the same kind of empathic concern for others.

There seems little question that the behavior of parents shapes the caring feelings and attitudes of children. According to the research of psychologists Nancy Eisenberg and Richard Fabes, parents who provide clear messages about the consequences for others of hurtful behaviors tend to have more empathic children. And parents who discuss emotions with children seem to have children with greater skills of sympathy and empathy.

If parents or other caretakers have little capacity for empathy or understanding another person's point of view, then children cannot learn by watching, nor do they have a model to imitate. Such children are limited in their ability to develop a repertoire of empathic responses to friends and acquaintances.

But if your teen has not developed a capacity for empathy, for one reason or another, or if you believe your adolescent is not as caring or feeling as he or she should be, then there are steps you can take to teach your teen to be more empathic.

SIX STEPS TO EMPATHY

1. Establish a genuine relationship.
2. Discuss feelings with your child.

3. Demonstrate caring behavior.

4. Provide consistent rules with clear consequences.

5. Use reasoning.

6. Teach the Golden Rule.

1. Establish a Genuine Relationship

When I teach empathy to teenagers, I am always conscious of demonstrating caring and kind behavior. I think that's where any adult can begin. When you show genuine care and concern for your child, you are beginning to give her the capacity for learning to care for other people.

So a first step is to form a solid relationship with your child. If you don't have a good relationship and if the adolescent doesn't feel you care for her, then you have to begin to build one and use it as a foundation in teaching. This is particularly important in this all-important social skill of having empathy for others.

A genuine relationship involves caring, support, encouragement, affection, acceptance, and the occasional setting of limits. For any adolescent to learn to be more empathic, she must feel loved and accepted and able to talk about feelings.

2. Discuss Feelings with Your Child

Empathic young people typically have parents who discuss their own feelings and encourage their children to talk about their feelings. You cannot hope to have a teenager who understands others' feelings if he's never had discussions about feelings. The language of feelings and emotions will be like a foreign language unless there is plenty of discussion around what is going on in the inner world of members of the family.

It's through talking about feelings that kids come to learn how others feel and are able to identify their own—and others'—feelings. The ability to identify their own feelings is a precursor to the skill of identifying the feelings of other people. And without this skill, there is no empathy.

3. Demonstrate Caring Behavior

If you consistently show your teen that you really care for her and work to build a strong relationship, then you have a base from which to set a positive example, and your teen will care about the example you're setting.

It's become a well-worn saying that children live what they learn, and it has a lot of truth behind it. Show your child about caring and empathy. Model it every day with your teen and in front of your teen. Care about the feelings of family, friends, colleagues, and neighbors, and there's a better chance that your child will follow your example.

When working with teenagers, I try to show a positive example of caring behavior in several ways:

First, I ask them about their feelings and respond to them in what I believe is a sensitive, feeling, and caring style. However, in some groups of adolescents when one member of the group relates an unfortunate incident, some of the other teens may laugh, giggle, or snicker. They might even say something rude or uncomplimentary, such as "It serves you right" or "That was a dumb thing to do."

No matter how ridiculous or unthinking the behavior of the teenager, I try to show my sympathy and concern for her. "That must have been upsetting," I might say, or "I would have felt very hurt if that had happened to me. How did you feel?"

Teenagers today experience much that is tragic, unsettling, or traumatic. Friends have bad experiences with drugs. Parents get divorced—and remarried. Parents get transferred to another city for work. Parents and siblings go to prison. Peers die in fatal accidents or are victims of firearm tragedies.

No matter what the trauma or stressful event, they must try to cope with it in some way. I often find in working with groups of adolescents that every teenager in a group will have experienced not just one but sometimes several traumatic events in their lives.

For instance, in a recent group, John, a 13-year-old boy, said he had had a bad week because a friend had been hit by a car and killed. I helped him to talk about his feelings by making empathic remarks and asking him questions. But then I turned to the other group members and asked how many others had also lost someone close to them. Every hand went up.

One boy had a friend who was shot. A girl had a cousin who died in a motorcycle accident. Another boy's father had been shot to death in a robbery. Still another teen had a friend who committed suicide.

I asked them how they dealt with their experiences and what they could share with John that would help him get through his ordeal. By initiating this discussion, I was able to help them label their feelings. I encouraged them to talk about both their experiences and their emotions, and I offered help as they wondered what to do about their lingering feelings.

I asked each member of the group to offer some supportive comment to another member. While this clearly made them uncomfortable, I thought it was important that they practice being empathic. Later that same day, the teenage boy who had lost his father remarked, "If we had Mr. Windell following us around all the time, we'd have to talk about our feelings and then we'd say and do the right thing." It was meant to be funny, and maybe even sarcastic, but he was also saying that as teenagers they needed a good role model to help them get along in emotional situations.

This kind of approach teaches teens how to use the language

of caring and empathy. Most of the teens with whom I work have not grown up speaking this language. So instead of responding to others in an empathic, feeling way, they are more likely to take a cold, even callous, approach when other people are hurting emotionally. But if they hear someone responding in a warm, caring way, they become more comfortable with this language and might begin to use it themselves.

Second, I ask adolescents about their feelings after I tell them my impression of their feelings: For example, I say, "You sound frustrated. How are you feeling today?" This approach is useful for troubled adolescents because they are not skilled at listening for the feelings of others. But I want them to learn to listen beneath the words that are being used so they can pick up on emotional tones and cues. Maybe if they get fairly good at this, they can begin to use it at home and with friends.

Third, I ask teens to practice making sensitive, supportive statements to others. That is one of the ways adolescents can earn extra credit in my groups—by making supportive, caring, complimentary comments to others. When someone does this, I point it out and give them positive feedback and praise. I want everyone else to recognize what was done well and how they, too, could practice the same behavior. While teenagers are typically uncomfortable giving positive, supportive feedback to others, with practice they can become quite skilled at this.

4. Provide Consistent Rules with Clear Consequences

As with other points in these six steps to teaching empathy, it's best if you begin in the early years of childhood and continue through adolescence. If you have been following through with consequences, don't stop now just because your child is gaining some independence. Simply adapt your rules and consequences. And if you haven't been doing this, it's better to start now than not at all.

You can *tell* your teen what's right and wrong, but you have to back up and practice what you preach through actions. Do you really believe that a certain behavior is wrong? Then be sure you have a clear rule about it, and enforce that rule with consistent consequences.

Adolescents know what you value and what behavior is important to you based not on what you say, but on your having rules and enforcing those rules through reasonable consequences and punishments. In this way their understanding of what is right and wrong gets reinforced. If you're willing to provide consequences for a misbehavior, then there's no guess work about whether you love them and wish them to adopt a certain code of behavior.

Even having rules and policies about showing caring behavior helps to set a tone and a standard for conduct. It tells teens what you value and that you care enough to establish standards and codes for their behavior.

And once a standard is established, you have to practice it, and you have to encourage them to practice it, especially when they forget or don't take the time to do so. If your general rule, for example, is that your child takes others' feelings into consideration, there are going to be times she may forget to do this or is too busy to remember. He may plan an activity with friends, forgetting that a younger cousin is coming to visit and was looking forward to spending time with him. Or you may overhear him dismiss a friend's efforts to share an upsetting experience with him. You can bring these lapses to your teen's attention later as you remind him of the feelings and needs of others: "Your cousin was so disappointed that you weren't here to share some time today. I think you owe him an apology."

5. Use Reasoning

When you tell your teen that specific behavior is right or wrong, you can use reasoning to help them understand why this is so. Reasoning means explaining why you set certain rules for your family. Reasoning works best if you include what I call a "victim impact statement": You let your kids know that the reason an action is right or wrong has to do with how it affects other people.

For instance, aggression is always wrong because it causes others pain. Stealing is always wrong because no one has a right to the belongings of another person. Malicious teasing is always wrong because it belittles someone.

Melissa, a 15-year-old, can be rather ruthless about her teasing of other teens who are younger, smaller, less intelligent, or even just different from her. When this happens in my presence, I tell her that's against the rules, and I give reasons why I don't want her to continue that behavior.

I can give those reasons in different ways. I can say, "How do you think she feels when you make fun of her for something she can't help?" Or I can say, "Melissa, when you tease LuAnn, you are calling attention to something that she already feels bad about. Your teasing makes her feel worse and that just isn't a kind thing to do."

Another approach I can take is to say, "Melissa, making fun of another person because she is smaller than you suggests that she isn't as good as you. That isn't fair, it hurts her feelings, and it's not the way people should be treated. I would like you to consider her feelings before you make fun of her."

When Melissa hears these reasons, she stops her teasing. When she has heard this kind of message often, I expect that she will think about the feelings of others before she starts to tease.

Taking a stand on such issues very clearly lets teens know

where you stand. At the same time the reasoning informs them as to why you take your position.

6. Teach the Golden Rule

We want our kids to be sensitive to other people. To be empathic means to put yourself in another's shoes: to feel as they feel. The Golden Rule—Do unto others as you would have them do unto you—teaches this concept. If your teen would like others to treat her with dignity and respect, then she must treat others in precisely this way.

As always in teaching our kids to be feeling, we ask them to be aware of how they might feel in the same situation. Once when my daughter found some money and said she intended to keep it, I asked her how she would feel if she had lost that amount of money and the person finding it made no effort to return it. She said she would feel bad. I said, "Then make sure you don't make some other person feel bad. Try as hard as you can to return this money."

When Jeremy was laughing behind the back of a janitor at his school because the man was severely physically disabled, his mother overheard. "Jeremy," she said, "I'm very disappointed in you for making fun of another human being. Because he is disabled doesn't make him less of a person. And, on top of that, life must be a real struggle for him. I want you to think about how much more difficult your life would be if you were disabled in the same way as he is."

"Ah, Mom, I was just kidding," Jeremy replied.

"Kidding or not," his mother said, "I am upset that you would think a person with his disabilities was funny. I'm serious about this, and I want you to write down some ways your life would be more difficult if you were born with his disabilities. And I want you to show me what you have come up with tomorrow."

By requiring Jeremy to think seriously about this issue and to reflect on how being disabled would change his life, his mother was forcing him to put himself in another person's position. When she saw his list the next day, she was impressed at what he had written on a piece of paper. Among the things he listed was this: "People might make fun of me behind my back and I wouldn't like it."

GOLDEN OPPORTUNITIES TO TEACH EMPATHY

There are, of course, many opportunities to practice empathy. Like Jeremy's mother, you can intervene when your teen shows a lack of empathy and give him an assignment that helps him to think differently about a situation.

You can do it in little ways, too. You can do it by being kind enough to rewind the tape every time you return a video to the video store. And you can do it by letting another car cut in front of you when you're driving or by using your mobile phone to call for help when another motorist is in distress.

Often, though, it's not enough to just model the behavior. We sometimes have to explain why we're doing it: "That person looks like she needs some help," you might say. Or "I've had a flat tire on a lonely highway and I know how it feels to be so helpless. So let's figure out a way we can help."

When our children were young, we took them to senior citizens' homes at Christmastime. We told them, "I'm sure that if we were living in a senior citizens' home, we would sometimes feel lonely, especially at the holidays. That's why we are going to try to brighten up an older person's holiday."

When my daughter was young, I worked at a juvenile court's detention center. I tried to speak of the kids living in the center with respect and empathy. Yes, I wanted her to know that they had been wrong to break the law, but I also wanted her to understand that they had feelings and often were sorry for their behavior. I always wanted her to understand that kids in detention centers were not faceless, anonymous monsters but children who missed out on having a nice home or loving parents.

When my children went to school, I wanted them to know that their teachers were people with feelings. I would share my own experiences as a teacher in a college and what it was like from the other side of the desk.

These days our world is rife with opportunities to teach empathy. It often seems that the newspapers and the TV news have stories everyday about children or teens who have acted in violent ways. Talking with our teens about how the victims of violence and aggression feel is a golden opportunity to teach an empathy lesson.

Another everyday situation that lends itself to empathy training concerns the new kids in class from Russia, Vietnam, Japan, China, Thailand, Mexico, or the Caribbean. We can discuss with our kids how they would feel if the situation were reversed and they were transported to Russia or to a southeast Asian country and started attending a public school. How would they feel? What would they hope others would say or do?

Let's say a teenage girl your child knows becomes pregnant or has a child. You can talk with your teen about the kinds of feelings a girl has when she discovers she's pregnant and the tough decisions she has to make. Will she have the baby? Will she keep it or give it up for adoption? What is it like to be a teenager and to raise a baby?

You hear of a teenager who experiences abuse or domestic violence. Ask your child to think about what it is like to grow up in such a home. How would your child feel? What would she experience? What if other people knew about it? How do you overcome it?

These situations, sadly so commonplace these days, are perfect opportunities to discuss how others feel and what they experience. Being aware of other's feelings will help your child become an adult of whom you can be proud.

PUTTING IT INTO ACTION

From the eight activities that follow, choose one or more that you can put into action with your teen.

1. To help your adolescent talk more openly about her feelings, use some of the feelings below to discuss which ones she's experienced. In discussing feelings, you can ask under what circumstances has she felt those she's experienced. Did she like the feelings? How did she cope with the feelings?

Sadness	Frustration
Happiness	Anger
Disappointment	Guilt
Weakness	Vulnerability
Triumph	Depression
Loneliness	Abandonment
Fear	Hatred
Joy	Surprise
Friendliness	Love

2. To help him better recognize the feelings of others, find situations in which you can ask your teen questions and discuss how others would feel in certain circumstances. Use the following questions as guidelines to help your discussion along:

- "How do you think she felt when she heard that?"
- "What must he be thinking now?"
- "What do you think was going through his mind when that happened?"

- "I'll bet she was scared. What do you think?"

- "How do you think they were feeling when they won?"

3. Give her feedback about her assessment or predictions about other's feelings. For instance, you can provide feedback in the following ways:

- "I would say he looked more disappointed."

- "If I were her I think I would be feeling very stressed out."

- "What I think she was feeling was helplessness."

4. Encourage your teen to give compliments to others. Help him train to get better at this. Do some of the following to help:

- Use role-playing to help him practice giving compliments.

- Rehearse ahead of an event so he has had an opportunity to practice giving a compliment.

- Model giving sincere and kind compliments in front of your teen, both to him and to other people.

- Vary the way you give compliments so he gets to hear many different ways of complimenting. For instance, use some of the following ways of complimenting:

  "Jim, you did a great job on that committee."

  "I really enjoyed your presentation last night."

  "That was a terrific golf shot. How did you learn to do that?"

  "I've always envied your ability to speak in front of a group."

5. Model showing appreciation to someone who has done something nice. Always use opportunities to demonstrate to your adolescent the fine art of saying thank you and expressing appre-

ciation. Use "thank yous" like the following examples to teach your teen to be kind to others:

- "Thank you for the nice bouquet you sent me. It was so sweet of you to think of me."
- "Thanks for offering to look after my puppy for me. That's really going out of your way, and I appreciate it."
- "That was so thoughtful of you to pick us up. I know you had to drive a long distance to help us out."

6. Ask your teen to keep a list of nice things she's done for others and whether she received a thank you. Ask her to explain how she felt when she got a sincere thank you versus when she did not.

7. Model offering help to others in front of your teen. Later discuss what you did and ask him how it makes him feel to offer help to others.

Also, ask him to tell you about the last time he offered to help someone. Then, discuss how he felt and how often he offers assistance to others. As part of the conversation, decide together how he could more frequently offer help to other people.

If he has difficulty offering help to others, discuss his feelings or attitudes that get in the way of his offering help. Discuss situations in which he might feel ambivalent or unsure of offering help (for instance, to a person in a wheelchair). Talk about what makes those situations so tough for him.

8. In your own life as a parent, make sure you follow the Golden Rule. Practice it and let your teen know that this is something you believe and practice often. Use it as a guideline in day-to-day life. When you or your teen are faced with a decision involving other people, remind her or him that the Golden Rule is a principle you should both try to follow.

6

STEP FIVE: TEACH YOUR TEENAGER TO HANDLE ANGER

Fourteen-year-old Kareem told me he got so angry at school that he beat up another boy, sending the other boy to the hospital. Kareem got suspended from school for ten days.

"This guy has been talking trash to me for weeks," Kareem said. "He was calling me names and told me he wanted to meet me in the parking lot after school. I told him no. But in the hallway, he started pushing me, and I lost it and started whaling on him. I got hauled down to the office and suspended from school."

Kevin, age 16, told me how he got angry at school recently. "The thing that gets to me is authority," Kevin said, "somebody telling me what to do. I hate that. This teacher came up to me in the lunchroom and told me to pick up a paper napkin that was on the floor. I said why should I because I didn't put it there. She said, 'Are you refusing to do what I'm telling you to do?' I said, 'Yeah,' and then I walked away." Kevin says that got him an after-school detention, which made him even more angry.

Amanda, 15, said that her blood boils when kids at her high school act tough. "Somebody acts all hard and tough, and I see red," Amanda said. "That really pushes my buttons. I just want to slap somebody like that. When I do, then I get in trouble."

It's Eric's stepfather who makes him mad. "It's like he thinks he's my dad or something," said 14-year-old Eric. "He tries to boss me around and tell me what time to come in, and I won't listen to him. I'll just go to my room and turn on my CDs really loud. That makes him mad, and he comes in and tells me to turn it down, and I tell him to get the fuck out of my room."

If these teenagers are at all typical of today's young people—and I think they are—it is obvious that many adolescents have considerable anger that gets triggered in various situations. Unfortunately, their knee-jerk ways of expressing their anger get them in trouble. Maybe it's not so much that teenagers are more angry these days, as that they go about expressing it in aggressive and violent ways that cause them so much difficulty and present the greatest concern for our society.

Good teenagers aren't those who never get angry—everyone gets angry at times. The healthy adolescent is the one who can handle anger without resorting to self-defeating aggression or violence. Anger itself is normal, but when the anger is too powerful, is too easily triggered, or leads to uncontrollable rages, or when the anger results in suspensions from school, fights with parents, friends, and peers, and trouble with the police, then it causes serious problems.

If your teen is too angry too often and doesn't seem to be able to control his behavior when angry, then you need to act. In the next several pages, I'll describe how you can teach your teenager to better control his or her anger and to express it in more appropriate and socially acceptable ways.

WHAT TRIGGERS YOUR TEEN'S ANGER?

Your kid needs to know that anger is a normal emotion and that, just as with any other feeling, there is nothing wrong with feeling angry. However, there is something wrong with anger that leads to aggression, hostility, and self-defeating behavior. When anger results in serious conflict with social norms and rules and interferes with the reaching of goals, it is a serious personal problem that must be approached like any other personal difficulty.

So they can better understand their anger, adolescents must talk about their angry emotions. To pave the way for this in my weekly groups of teenagers, we often begin a unit on discussion of anger management by watching a video. I like to use a video called "Just Chill! Dealing with Anger." Although this video has some limitations as a teaching film, it is a good, dramatic, and contemporary overview of some of the problems teens frequently face.

In four vignettes in the video, teenagers are seen in typical situations that lead to anger. In one, a teen hears that one of his best friends has been asking the teen's girlfriend out. He must confront them both, but in the process he loses control of his temper. In another vignette, a teenage girl misses out on dates because she has to babysit for her little brother while her hard-working, single mother works nights. She thinks she's angry at the behavior of her preschool brother, when she's really angry with her mother for robbing her of part of her adolescence. In a third vignette, an adolescent girl gets even with a drugstore manager who accuses her of stealing by shoplifting articles from his store. Finally, the last vignette shows a high school boy who turns to drugs and alcohol to express his anger after losing his job when a grocery store goes out of business.

Each of these vignettes contains something with which most teens can easily identify, and each makes a somewhat different point about anger. As a whole, the video allows for discussion about such key concepts as misplaced anger, acting out of anger, feeling powerless at a situation one can't change, and some methods of coping with anger (such as taking deep breaths and channeling the negative emotion into positive action).

Watching the video helps the teens in my groups talk about their own experiences with anger—some very similar to what they saw in the video. And that's the starting point for them to admit their anger aloud. Having confessed they don't always handle their anger well, it's easier to go on in later weeks to discuss specifics of their anger problems. That's a key first step—getting your teenager to talk openly about her anger. You may also want to find a video or a movie that shows a person who has problems with his anger. In the Resources section, I recommend some videos you may wish to order.

Of course, your adolescent may have nowhere near the same kinds of difficulties with anger control as do the kids in my groups, but most teenagers at one time or another will have some control problems, and you will be giving a wonderful gift by teaching your child how to handle this powerful emotion.

A FORMAT FOR TEACHING TEENS ABOUT ANGER

It helps if you have a simple format in mind to guide you in the process of teaching your teen about anger. The following three-step anger-management process can help:

1. Recognizing Anger Triggers
2. Learning about Anger Styles
3. Teaching Anger-Management Methods: Nine Healthy Ways to Deal with Anger

As I have said, the initial step is to get your child to talk about her anger and admit she sometimes has a problem with it. In the beginning, emphasize that it's a normal emotion and that "everyone" feels very angry at some times. You can point to times you've been angry to emphasize this point. But it usually works better if you don't use examples of being angry with her! Pick another target.

RECOGNIZING ANGER TRIGGERS

What makes one person angry doesn't necessarily set off the next person. We all have our own triggers—those things that make us mad. When I ask teenagers what their triggers are, they tell me things like these:

"It's stupid people who make me mad," said one adolescent. "I can't stand really stupid people who say stupid things."

"What makes me angry is teachers who pick on me," said another teen. "It's like the whole class can be talking, but a teacher will pick me out and send me to the office. It's not fair. That's why I get mad and swear at teachers."

"I get really mad when I get in trouble for things I didn't do," said a teenage girl.

"I'll tell you what makes me mad," said another adolescent girl. "It's my mom. She always tells me I'm in trouble. She says that so much I want to blow her head off."

"My little sister gets to me and makes me go crazy," said a 14-year-old girl. "She makes up things about me, and my dad believes her. She's little miss perfect and I'm the screw-up."

"It's somebody calling you a name," added a 16-year-old boy. "That makes me boil. I hate names like four-eyes, queer, or fag. I feel like kicking the shit out of someone who calls me a name like that."

Teenagers usually admit that they have trouble handling it when someone calls them a name. For most of the teenage boys I work with, being called a "fag" is about the worst possible insult they can imagine. That's a fighting word. However, there are some names and epithets that bother some teens but can be laughed off by others. Being ordered around by an adult will bother most teens, and being nagged by a parent can drive some kids wild. But not every adolescent is supersensitive to orders, instructions, or requests from adults. For those who are, however, this trigger results in anger that can get them into serious trouble when they refuse to obey.

Helping your child identify some of his personal triggers and helping him recognize how he reacts to them is important. It's an initial step in using his mind to get better control of this emotion. I like to have kids keep a log of some of their triggers. Being able to make a list of the things that really tick them off is very important because it increases their self-awareness and self-understanding.

LEARNING ABOUT ANGER STYLES

When 16-year-old Caren gets angry, she becomes depressed and withdrawn. She is likely to stop eating, adopts a negative, fatalistic attitude, and complains that she has no energy. She views the world as hopeless, and she is convinced that nothing she can say or do will solve the problem. If Caren is angry with her boyfriend's mother, for instance, she might say, "There's no use in talking to her because her mind is made up. She's just a bitch, and I just won't talk to her anymore."

Fifteen-year-old Alex handles his anger in a different way. He gets mad quickly and easily, often taking offense at a slight hardly noticed by anyone else. He flies off the handle, says mean, offensive things, and within fifteen or twenty minutes is cooled off. He's ready to resume the relationship, and he can't understand why the person he yelled at is still upset. "Look," he says, "I'm sorry. You know how I get mad, but I don't mean what I say. So just forget about it, okay?" However, neither his stepmother nor his girlfriend can forget what he said so quickly.

Like Caren and Alex, every adolescent has his or her own anger style. A person's anger style shows what she does and how she reacts when she gets angry. Some teenagers will react instantly with hostility and aggression when they're angry. Others will withdraw and or deny they're mad. Still others need to talk about it when they're mad and will seek you out and spill their guts letting you know exactly what the problem is. Some kids are confrontive, wanting to clear the air when they're angry with you, and others are passive, finding any kind of talk about their feelings difficult or very uncomfortable.

My two children, Jill and Jason, reflect totally different styles in the way they handle their anger. This was even true when they were toddlers and preschoolers. Jill was the kind of child who needed to let you know that she was very happy or very angry. She could express joy, sadness, or love, but she also always let us know when she was unhappy. If she was angry, she couldn't hold it in and needed to talk about it to resolve the source of the anger. If bothered by a problem—whether it related to her anger or to another feeling—she'd let us know and try to get it settled.

Jason, on the other hand, always kept his angry feelings more closely guarded. As a toddler he would withdraw, pout, and re-treat into his private thoughts. As a teenager, he would look mad or unhappy, but he couldn't talk about his feelings until he had had a long time to think about them and figure things out. If he needed to, he could put on a social face and amiable appearance while he was seething inside. Only later, based on his withdraw-ing and not talking, would you know he was really mad. Even then, he could not confront. He wanted to keep things pleasant and cordial because he didn't feel comfortable with his angry feelings. Their different styles required different responses. We had to work harder to draw Jason out to a point where he'd feel comfortable sharing feelings.

The teenagers I've worked with through most of my career have had their various styles of dealing with their anger, too.

Because a great many of the adolescents I've dealt with had problems with anger and aggression, they tended to be quicker to express their anger and more impulsive in their reactions than my own children. They were more likely to seek revenge, to act out their anger, or to take it out on others.

Often these approaches to anger will mean that anger is never confronted in a direct, verbal way. Instead there is an instant blowup with aggressive reactions or denial of anger and later acting out—through revenge or taking it out on someone (maybe even the wrong person).

I use six different categories of anger styles. The descriptions that follow will help you identify your child's style and learn how best to respond to it.

1. The Rocket

One of the most difficult types of teens is The Rocket, who expresses his anger with a big blast and fireworks. Psychologists call this acting out. Teenagers like this respond quickly, often because they are impulsive and in many instances already have plenty of bottled up anger from past years of hurt. They seem to be full of rage and sometimes instantly react with vengeance. This, of course, means they don't talk about their anger—they just act on it.

Seventeen-year-old Phil was a Rocket. He was at home with his girlfriend Melissa and her friend Maria. Phil, who tends to be controlling with Melissa, was upset that Melissa wanted to go to a movie with Maria. They started arguing about whether she would go. As the argument got more heated, Maria thought they both might get violent and called 911. Within a few minutes, a squad car arrived.

When Phil and Melissa saw the police drive up in front of the house, they walked outside. The police talked to them, trying to settle them both down. Phil could not cool his anger because

Melissa wouldn't agree not to go to the movie. The police asked Phil to go into the house.

"No, why should I?" retorted Phil.

"Because I asked you to," the officer replied.

"You can't tell me what to do on my property," Phil said belligerently.

"I think you'd be better off going in the house and calming down," the officer said.

"I'm not going anywhere," Phil said.

At this point another patrol car arrived, and two more officers walked toward the scene in the front yard of the house.

"If you don't calm down and go in the house," the original officer said, "I'll have no choice but to arrest you."

"You don't have any right coming in here and telling me what to do," Phil said angrily.

All three officers walked toward him. One officer took out his handcuffs and reached for Phil's wrists. Phil pulled his hand and arm away and began swearing at the officers. Despite his resistance, Phil was quickly subdued and arrested. The charge against him was resisting arrest, and he spent a night in jail before his father bailed him out.

Like Phil, adolescents who act out their anger often go too far, which can sometimes cause serious personal problems. And if you are the parent of a teenager who acts out her anger in an impulsive manner, you have your work cut out for you in terms of teaching her to manage her anger in a more controlled and appropriate way.

Yet, it can be done, so don't give up. One of the problems in teaching a Rocket to better handle her anger is that the outbursts are quick and soon over. Rockets don't often want to talk about what's in the past (even if that past is only a few hours ago), so it's difficult to find an opportunity that provides a teachable moment. I'll say more about this later in the chapter when I discuss golden opportunities to teach about anger management.

2. The Avenger

Thirteen-year-old Carlos stole money from his father's wallet. When the theft of the money was discovered, Carlos said he did it because he was mad and wanted to get back at his father. Carlos is an Avenger.

"My dad took away my computer," Carlos said, "and I didn't think he had any right to do that so I took something from him."

Teenagers who seek revenge are often those who carry a grudge or brood about their anger for long periods of time. They will do something at sometime to get even for the anger they feel.

When they're angry, they plot about how they'll get even. "I'll get him sometime when his back is turned," said one teenager whose predominant style is to seek revenge.

Avengers will deny their anger, yet you can be fairly sure that he is plotting revenge if you saw him get angry. Try to draw him out by confronting him about the plotting going on in his mind. That will be disarming, and when he knows you understand him, he will be more likely to share his angry feelings.

3. The Crab

Misplaced anger can come about for various reasons. Some teens take their anger out on the wrong person because they can't confront the person who really made them angry or because they've been carrying around a lot of hurt for a long time. This type is the Crab.

George, 15, is a Crab. He says he can't show his mother the anger he has toward her. He's not sure why, but one possible reason is that she would punish him severely if he raised his voice or said anything that she regarded as "hateful." George, therefore, restrains his anger toward her, but he's still angry. Instead he takes it out on his girlfriends, each of whom he calls a "ho."

Seemingly bitter toward all girls and women, George does not see that this might be related to his mother. "They're all gold diggers," he says of girls. And he adds, "You can't trust any girl 'cause they go behind your back with their gossip."

If your teen is a Crab, be sure you don't take her anger personally when it's directed at you. Instead try to point out what you think she's really mad about and encourage her to talk about her real anger.

4. The Clam

Some adolescents can't stand the thought of beginning to express all the anger they feel. Clams are fearful that if they start to let it out, maybe there would be no controlling their rage. Therefore, it's safer to clam up and hold it inside.

Sometimes this style has developed because it really was unsafe to express how they felt as they were growing up. There are a couple of possible reasons for this.

One is fear of losing a parent's love. Melissa, at 13, is fearful of expressing her anger or upset around her father. Her parents were divorced when she was four, and she was always unsure of her father's love for her. Because he was rather unstable and volatile, she never felt secure in letting him know about unpleasant feelings. She's afraid of telling him when he does something to make her mad. She's afraid she might never see him again if she really let him know how she felt.

Another reason for being a Clam is not wanting to rock the boat. Dion doesn't show anger around his mother. A fragile woman with many insecurities of her own, she cannot handle the strong feelings of others. Long before he became a teenager, Dion figured out that it was best to keep his feelings under control. His mother's overreactions and depression taught him that hiding his feelings and swallowing his anger kept things in his family more tranquil.

Both Dion and Melissa have developed the style of holding their anger in. If your teen is a Rocket, you may think that it would be easier to have a Clam in your house. Actually, though, it's much easier to deal with a Rocket because his anger is out in the open, and he will usually admit to having a problem. In that respect, it's easier to deal with a child who explodes in rage. A Clam is harder to figure out and often those teens who hold on to their anger are less likely to admit they have a problem.

Even if your Clam doesn't admit to his anger, you can help by reassuring him that he can feel safe in expressing whatever he feels. Make sure you're willing to accept his angry feelings so that when he starts to express them he doesn't have to pull back and clam up again.

5. The Denier

The Denier, like the Clam, withholds feelings but also is in need of being in control of situations. Adolescents who need to stay in control often deny that they're angry. They'll deny it to others and even to themselves. To admit it would be admitting they have flaws or would represent such a loss of control that they couldn't accept themselves. They tend to be more perfectionistic and as a result just deny that they're angry.

Matt, age 13, seems angry often, but he denies it.

"What are you mad about?" his mother asks.

"Nothing," replies Matt. "I'm not mad. Maybe a little tired. I get grumpy sometimes. But I'm not angry about anything."

Yet, his mother experiences him as almost constantly angry. And she says he has good reason to be mad. His father, who is divorced from his mother, has recently begun living with a woman who has a 13-year-old son. Matt doesn't like this boy who has moved in on his territory. But when his mother asks him if what his father has done bothers him, Matt says no.

Matt believes he is not angry about this new boy in his life and in his father's home. He says it doesn't bother him. Yet he remains grumpy and irritable.

Like other teens who deny anger, Matt may not be aware of how angry he is about the experiences in his life. He may not want to deal with his anger, or he may not want to risk losing the affection of his father. Whatever the reason, he is not in touch with his anger—even when it is very clear to his mother that he is mad most of the time.

Because Deniers are not in touch with their feelings, you have to teach them how to label feelings accurately before they can actually express them. Sometimes you need to correct them when they put the wrong name—like grumpiness or fatigue—to a feeling.

6. The Confronter

Sara is a Confronter. She had worked very hard to get on the honor roll. She knew the day her report card was to arrive in the mail, and she hurried home to open up the envelope to see her great results.

However, after ripping the envelope open, she was shocked to see that her grade in history was a C.

"I got a C!" Sara exclaimed aloud. "I can't believe Mrs. Wallace would do this to me. I turned in every assignment and even did an extra-credit report."

She could hardly wait for her mother to come home from work so she could show her the report card. Her mother was barely in the door before Sara stuck the report card in her face.

"Look at this would you!" Sara said loudly. "I'm really mad. I thought for sure I was going to get all As and Bs. Look at this," and she pointed at the history grade.

"Wait a minute," her mother said. "Let's calm down and let

me sit down and look at your report card." With Sara following her, she went into the dining room and sat down in a chair.

Together they looked over the report card, and her mother made positive comments about the other grades. When they talked about her C in history, she asked Sara what she was going to do.

"I'm going to talk to Mrs. Wallace tomorrow," she said. "I'm going to ask her why I got this grade. I know I deserved a B."

The Confronter probably has the healthiest style. That should be the goal for your teen if she presently uses one of the other anger styles. We want teens to talk about their anger and to confront situations in an assertive way when necessary.

When Russ heard that another boy at school was telling kids that Russ got drunk at a high school football game, he was furious. But being a Confronter, he went to the boy and told him they needed to talk.

"I don't know where you got your information," Russ said to the boy. "But for your information, I don't drink and I've never been drunk. I don't appreciate you going around telling people things about me that aren't true."

Russ's assertive confrontation with the rumor-spreading boy stopped those rumors very quickly.

If your teen uses another style, try to teach her to be a Confronter. One of the benefits of this style is that when she tells people what they did to make her mad, she will be empowered and more self-confident. If your teen is already a Confronter, make sure you teach her the assertive techniques you already know from Chapter 4 to be sure she is confronting appropriately.

The important thing for any teen, regardless of his anger style, is that he learn about the way he expresses his anger. Although insight and self-knowledge are generally important for growth and personal development, when it comes to anger, the more a teenager knows about himself and his anger the better.

In order to control anger, it is essential that a teen know precisely how he typically expresses angry feelings and be able to talk about it. If teens are going to make any positive changes, they need to know how they act now and what they need to do to change.

The teen who reacts impulsively needs to learn to control her impulses. The teen who withdraws must work on sticking with an angry situation and resolving it before too much time has lapsed. The teen who denies his anger and keeps it from others must learn to be more open and honest with his feelings.

But how do you teach teens to do this? Part of the answer comes in what we've been talking about. Help them to be familiar with their anger styles. Talk about anger styles in your family. Label everybody's anger style, and be candid about your own. If your anger and the style you employ cause you problems, admit it. Show how you've tried—or succeeded—in making changes yourself. Telling about your own experiences during adolescence with your anger could help.

When I tell adolescents about my own problems handling anger, they have trouble believing it: "You mean you didn't always talk about how you felt? Come on. You're just saying that."

Then I have to admit I wasn't very good at handling anger when I was their age. "I'd get all mad inside and then go off by myself and think about how mad I was instead of talking about it. That hurt my relationships with my parents, my friends, and my girlfriends because no one could figure out why I was mad. I knew it and I could write about it, but I couldn't say it out loud to anyone."

The important message I want to get across to them is that by looking at my own anger style and how it hurt me, I learned to change. It wasn't comfortable staying the way I was.

On the other hand, I can freely admit that changing is no fun. *Change* inevitably requires giving up familiar and comfortable practices and moving into new behaviors, which is scary and takes courage. I challenge them to summon up their courage and to do what is difficult to do. "It's not easy to change," I'll say by way of challenge, "but I think you can do it."

When I'm working with adolescents, I want kids to say aloud and in front of others what their anger style is. That's a first step— admitting it and saying it out loud. Then, I want them to list some of the disadvantages of their particular style.

A Rocket displays the impulsive, raging style that gets kids into trouble. They've been locked up or suspended from school or on probation as a result of this style. Deniers carry around considerable anger and bad feelings that sometimes come out in antisocial ways. The delinquents I see in groups often can identify with this style. They know they've been hurt and disappointed by authority figures throughout their life. They're angry at not being able to trust anyone.

And the Clam usually carries the burden of disrupted relationships. These disruptions often don't get resolved. By withdrawing and keeping anger hidden, the Clam never solves the real problem.

Teenagers can usually see these disadvantages to their styles. Counting up the disadvantages helps to inspire them to learn more about anger management and to make changes. The real changes can occur when they learn more about intervention methods.

TEACHING ANGER-MANAGEMENT METHODS: NINE HEALTHY WAYS TO DEAL WITH ANGER

Adolescents can use a number of appropriate anger-management approaches. I use nine different management methods that I've found best help teenagers handle their anger constructively:

1. Assertive confrontation
2. Breathing techniques for relaxation
3. Progressive relaxation
4. Autogenic Training
5. Visualization
6. Listening to soothing and quieting music
7. A cognitive approach: Stop and Think
8. Exercise and physical activity
9. Changing negative feelings into positive action

I will take these one at a time and explain how to teach them to your adolescent.

1. Assertive Confrontation

I already mentioned that my daughter Jill tended to be a confrontive person who didn't like to let problems fester. I can recall a time when she was 15. She and her brother Jason rode the same bus, usually crowded with mostly middle school and high school students, to and from school. She noticed that some older kids who rode the bus were picking on Jason.

Not one to shrink from confrontation, Jill got on the bus one morning, stood just behind the driver, put her hands on her hips, and made an announcement for everyone to hear: "If any of you has a problem with my brother, come and see me about it. But leave him alone!" Nobody came to Jill with the problem, and he wasn't picked on after that.

Confrontive? Yes. Assertive? Most definitely. Bordering on aggressiveness? No doubt. But the point was made. Jill didn't want to hear about anyone picking on her little brother (never mind that she picked on him at times!).

Like most teens who confront problems head on, she was not one to brood about things that were bothering her. Generally, it's healthy for teenagers to deal with problems directly; and when they're angry, they should talk about it or deal with it in an assertive style. In Chapter 4, I described the differences between assertive, passive, and aggressive interpersonal styles. The goal is to teach your teenager to be able to be assertive while avoiding aggression when she's angry.

When your adolescent has learned to be assertive, he can use this skill when he is angry, which is when teens tend to resort to aggressive, hostile, and violent actions. Teens should understand that it is okay to be angry, but it is not okay to be aggressive, threatening, or hostile.

Sean is an adolescent who has learned to use assertiveness well. He recently had a confrontation in an office where he works part-time. A manager in the office accused Sean of mishandling a memo, one that Sean had typed and distributed as he had been directed by another manager.

Sean looked the accusing manager in the eye and said, "I don't think this is the way things are handled in this office. Let's ask someone else to clear this up and verify which of us is right."

When Sean stood up to him in this assertive way, the manager, who was furious with Sean at first, backed down and agreed to allow another person in the department to give his opinion about the correct office practices.

Sixteen-year-old Christie was employed during the summer to run errands in a law office. One of the attorneys demanded that Christie come in early to type a brief. The attorney gave her the order in an aggressive, insulting way. Christie stayed calm and said pleasantly but firmly, "That's not my job, and those aren't my hours. You're demanding a favor. I have no problem doing a favor, but you can't tell me to do you a favor. Ask me in a polite way, and I'll be glad to do it." The partner backed down and asked politely. Christie quickly assented to do him the favor.

Neither Sean nor Christie had to get aggressive. In fact if they had, they could have been fired. Being assertive helped them to avoid this and to keep on good terms with fellow employees, while still standing up for themselves.

Assertiveness is particularly important for the Rocket, the Crab, and the Confronter to learn.

2. Breathing Techniques for Relaxation

It would be great if all kids were taught various relaxation methods when they were young. But, of course, that doesn't happen. Actually, many adults are not adept in using methods of relaxation to help them when they're anxious, stressed, or angry.

One of the easiest such methods to teach an adolescent is to take deep breaths. Many people, particularly athletes, seem to hit on this themselves and use it in stressful situations. If you watch any amount of NBA basketball, you'll notice that basketball players, when a free throw is particularly important, stand at the free throw line, eye the basket, and take a series of slow breaths, working their diaphragm as they breathe in and out. The same procedure is critical in teaching a teen to control stress, frustration, or anger.

To use breathing most effectively, start from the abdomen and inhale deeply, filling the lungs and expanding the chest. When your lungs are filled, hold it a few seconds and then exhale slowly. Then repeat this process two or three times.

This simple method, which can be combined with counting (you can teach a teen to count slowly from one to three as he inhales and from four to six as he exhales), will bring about relaxation. As the adolescent concentrates on the breathing process, the mind is diverted from the source of frustration or anger—at least for several seconds. As a self-calming effect takes place, the person is more likely to think rationally and is less inclined to act irrationally or impulsively.

Encourage your adolescent to use this method when she is getting too frustrated or angry and when she sees that someone else is getting under her skin. For example, Mandy was being taunted by some other girls as she walked along the hallway at school.

"Nice going on the algebra test, Mandy," one girl said. "What'd you get on it? Another E?"

"Yeah," chimed in another girl, "when you going to pass a test? You'll never get out of Algebra I the way you're going. What a loser!"

Mandy, already feeling bad after failing another math test, didn't need to be taunted about it. She was starting to go into a slow boil. But she also began to remember what she had learned about using deep breaths to control frustration and anger. As she walked toward her next class, she concentrated on taking several slow, deep breaths. She used her paces to count as she slowly inhaled and then slowly exhaled. By doing this, she was paying more attention to her breathing than to what the girls behind her were saying. Mandy was able to get to her next class without getting mad and losing control.

Breathing procedures can be especially helpful for the Rocket, the Avenger, and the Clam.

3. Progressive Relaxation

One of the best relaxation procedures is deep-muscle relaxation, commonly called progressive relaxation. This method takes practice and a certain amount of dedication, but I've found that teens can learn to utilize it to their advantage.

The essence of progressive relaxation, pioneered by renowned physician Edmund Jacobson, is the releasing of unwanted tension by alternately tensing and relaxing major muscles. With this deceptively simple technique, any adolescent, with practice, can learn to control stress, tension, and anger while achieving a state of calmness and relaxation whenever it's needed.

I have taught this method to adolescents in individual sessions, in group therapy, and in classrooms. And although teenagers typically feel embarrassed about trying this in the first demonstration session, they can become more comfortable with it and can then practice it in private at home.

With the help of various audiotapes (which are listed under Resources), you can teach your adolescent what happens in progressive relaxation and how this procedure can help him. The next step is to show him how to tense and relax a few common muscles, like the forearms or biceps.

After introducing the technique, ask your teen to sit in a comfortable chair, with the lighting subdued. Suggest that he get comfortable and close his eyes while following the instructions on the audiotape. You can supervise this first practice session and follow the procedure yourself so the teen doesn't feel that you're making him do something you wouldn't do.

Almost all instructors in this method give instructions that sound like this: "I want you to make a fist with your right hand. Make a tight fist . . . hold it . . . and now let go. Open your hand and let it rest comfortably on the arm of the chair . . . Now, make a fist after bringing your right hand up close to your shoulder. Flex your biceps muscle . . . hold it . . . and now relax. . . relax that muscle."

After you've done the 15-to-20-minute procedure that goes through all the major muscles in the body together, ask your child to use the tape twice a day for about two weeks to practice the procedure. Following this, most teens who have been practicing will be adept enough at the procedure that they can be aware when muscles in their body are tense and they can automatically relax them by thinking about those muscles and making sure that they are not being tensed. With practice, most people can in just a few seconds mentally do a check of their muscles and relax any that feel tense.

As with abdominal breathing, deep-muscle relaxation can be used any time tension, frustration, or anger threatens to take control of your teen. At first, however, while your teen is still practicing and learning progressive relaxation (or the next method, autogenic training), it will seem totally impractical to her. When teens think of anger, they think of getting mad at someone, having an urge to fight them, and having to deal with the problem *now*.

But there are many other kinds of situations where they need to get their anger under control. For example, frustration and anger builds over time when they have a friend who frequently lets them down, when they have asked to go on an overnight camping trip in two weeks but you've said no the first couple of times it's been brought up, or when they are consistently being humiliated by a teacher.

Such situations call for a relaxation method that will allow them to keep their angry emotions under control. Anger types who can benefit from this approach are the Rocket, the Avenger, and the Crab.

4. Autogenic Training

Autogenic training is a relaxation technique that was devised by the German psychiatrist Johannes Schultz. It combines elements of auto-suggestion, self-hypnosis, meditation, and exercise of the imagination.

As in self-hypnosis, the individual directs his attention away from the external environment and focuses on body sensations of heaviness and warmth. When the body feels warm and heavy, the body and its muscles are more likely to be relaxed.

As with progressive relaxation, you will need to buy an audiotape (options are given in the Appendix) that your teen can listen to so he has the instructions readily at hand. Typical instructions for autogenic training guide the individual to "feel your right hand getting heavy." The instructions, often accompanied by soothing music, give the suggestions that certain parts of the body (usually hands, arms, abdomen, and legs) are becoming warm as well as heavy. The breathing is to be slow and deep. Various muscles of the body are to become limp and relaxed. The pulse is to be calm and steady.

With suggestions of heaviness and warmth, teens usually become very relaxed and sometimes fall asleep. Afterward, they often describe the sensations as being hypnotized or feeling very sleepy.

With daily practice, adolescents will learn to relax more effectively. After many practices, they find that they can use this in real-life situations.

Miles, a 14-year-old who played baseball, was excited about playing on a new team. His mother insisted he keep afternoon appointments with a therapist before he went to practice. Miles, however, was worried about being late to practice and wanted to cancel his weekly appointment. His mother insisted, and they got into an argument with Miles refusing to get out of the car when they arrived at the therapist's office.

"I'm not going in and you can't make me," Miles said to his mother.

"If you don't keep your appointment," his mother replied, "you're not going to baseball practice at all today."

He sat stonily in the front seat, refusing to budge. His mother got out and went into the building to summon the therapist. The therapist returned to the car with her and coaxed Miles into the office. Once in the office, however, Miles was so angry he could barely talk.

When the therapist asked about other problems with his mother lately, Miles said, "I'm so pissed off at her I can't even talk."

Instead of trying to carry on a conversation, the therapist used autogenic training with Miles. This was a technique the therapist had just recently introduced into the weekly sessions because Miles had frequent problems with his anger. The therapist played an autogenic tape, and Miles gladly listened to the tape and complied with the taped instructions because he didn't have to talk.

As the therapist watched Miles following the guided auto-genic-training tape, he could see Miles's body become relaxed and less rigid. Miles soon closed his eyes and was breathing deeper and in a more relaxed way. At the end of the 20-minute tape, Miles was relaxed and had none of the palpable anger he had projected previously. They were able to talk about Miles using this method whenever he got too angry with his mother.

The Rocket and the Avenger can profit from learning this procedure.

5. Visualization

Visualization is often combined with another relaxation method, such as progressive relaxation. Once the teen is less tense and more relaxed, she can then work on her anger through visualization, or imagining a quiet, relaxing scene.

There are many audiotapes that teach you to visualize through spoken descriptions of imaginary scenes and "journeys." The basic concept is simple and always pretty much the same. The listener is told to imagine a scene that is pleasant and relaxing, taking you away from the anger or stress of the moment.

When I teach adolescents to fantasize or to use a visualization process to relieve tension, anger, and stress, I ask them to sit comfortably, to close their eyes, and to imagine being in an idealized location. I describe a place like a seashore or a forest or the deck of a Caribbean cruise ship. I use many details in describing the warm temperature, the lazy, white clouds, the rolling waves of the ocean, and the bright sunshine that warms their body.

By learning to get away to a fantasy spot, adolescents can return to this relaxing place whenever they need to. As a parent, you can teach your teen to have and use a fantasy escape whenever she is too tense or angry.

It is often the Rocket, the Avenger, and the Clam who can especially use this technique.

6. Listening to Soothing and Quieting Music

Unfortunately, these days a lot of teenagers, particularly those with anger problems, think that they relax by listening to heavy metal rock or rap music. Of course, such music is not at all relaxing or soothing—it's anything but calming.

One of the things we have to teach adolescents about music is what is quieting and soothing—not that I'm trying to change their musical taste, although I often wish I could. At best, I'm attempting to let them know about the difference between music that is soothing and calming and music that is exciting, pulsating, and energizing. I don't have anything against exciting music, but teens need to recognize that if they choose to try to use music to relax and to reverse the effects of anger, they must choose the right kind of music.

Some good choices are New Age music, classical music, and "easy listening" popular music. Especially good for relaxing away anger are classical compositions by Beethoven ("Moonlight Sonata" and portions of his famous symphonies), Brahms (Symphony No. 3, the third movement), Debussy ("Claire de Lune" and *Prelude to the Afternoon of a Faun*), Aaron Copland (*Appalachian Spring*), Tchaikovsky (*Swan Lake, Sleeping Beauty,* and the overture to *Romeo and Juliet*), and Johann Strauss ("Blue Danube" and other waltzes). So are such popular New Age artists as George

Winston ("Autumn" is a representative recording), whose piano features a relaxing, soothing sound. Easy listening music, such as orchestral renditions of the Beatles' songs, Nat King Cole ballads, and music by Harry Connick Jr., is also relaxing.

Teens who fly off the handle quickly, such as the Rockets, will benefit from this method of controlling anger. If Confronters need to calm down and think about the best way to approach a situation before doing any confronting, soothing music may be the answer.

7. A Cognitive Approach: Stop and Think

In cognitive approaches to dealing with anger, teens are taught to think about what is happening to them and how they ought to best proceed. One of the best "Stop and Think" approaches you can teach is this one:

- Stop and ask yourself: What's making me angry?
- Then ask: What are ways I can handle this?
- Analyze the ways you've come up with and try the best one.
- Ask yourself: How did I do, and could I have handled this better?

It's a simple process, yet teens who learn this skill must be able to remember it early enough when they're angry that they'll not only use it but remember to follow all the steps. It is important for adolescents to know that even those who handle their anger in impulsive ways can benefit from this technique.

Drake was a 17-year-old who had been on probation for fighting and other delinquent behavior. After learning this Stop and Think approach, he described how he used it at school one day when a teacher made a joke in front of the class about

Drake's ponytail. Drake considered the teacher's joke offensive and provocative.

"I remembered we had learned to stay calm and to think about what the problem was," Drake said in recounting the incident. "So I stayed cool even though the teacher really made me angry. I then started thinking, just like we had learned, 'What's the problem?' Of course, I knew that he was making a joke about me and maybe trying to get me to react.

"So I then thought about how I could handle it. One of the things that came to me was to just stay calm and not say anything because if I said anything back I could get into trouble. I just started looking at my assignment from yesterday and didn't say one word. The teacher dropped it, and he let me alone."

Drake had successfully used the Stop and Think approach by following the steps he had learned. He wouldn't have been able to handle this kind of situation before. In fact, he had described several times when people had made fun of him and he'd responded angrily or started fights.

Jerome, age 16, is a star player on his high school basketball team. Although he liked to joke around, all of his friends knew that he had a quick temper. This was especially true on the basketball court. Jerome takes basketball very seriously, and that includes the trash talk that typically goes on in high school basketball rivalries.

One of the players on a crosstown high school team has been playing against Jerome in school sports for four years starting in middle school. In recent games when they have guarded each other, the other boy, Nate, teased and baited Jerome by making sarcastic and cutting remarks.

In one game when Jerome was not playing his best, Nate's patter was getting to Jerome. When Nate made a comment about Jerome's mother, Jerome threw the ball at Nate, bouncing it off his head. Nate responded by diving headlong into Jerome's midsection knocking him to the hardwood floor. Jerome started swinging, and both were pulled apart by the referees and teammates. Although neither was ejected, they were given fouls and benched by their respective coaches.

"I couldn't help it," Jerome said later to the coach. "He kept pushing me and pushing me, and finally I couldn't take it anymore."

"But Jerome," the coach said, "I can't let a hothead start for me. If you didn't get ejected this time, you were lucky. Maybe you won't be so lucky next time. You've got to learn to control your anger. Don't you realize that players like Nate know you'll get angry when they talk trash and that they do it on purpose to throw your whole game off?"

"I know, coach," Jerome countered. "But he has no right to say those things to me. Anybody would get mad."

"I don't know about anybody," the coach replied. "I just know about you and the kind of player I want on my team. You've got to learn to handle your anger."

"But how do I do that?" asked Jerome. "I can't help but get mad when someone keeps pushing me."

"That attitude's the first thing that has to go," the coach said. "Trust me when I tell you that many players that I've coached over the years had tempers like yours. But all of the best ones learned to control their tempers and not let trash talk get to them."

"I guess I believe you, coach," Jerome said tentatively, "but how do I handle it when I'm out there in a game?"

"Here's what you have to do," the coach said. "Think about what you're trying to do and what someone like Nate is trying to do. You're trying to play your best game, and he's attempting to make you play less than your best. Right?"

"Right," agreed Jerome.

"Now, you have to tell yourself that he is talking trash that gets to you on purpose. He knows what gets to you, and he's going to use that. But you have to be smarter. You have to say to your-self, 'I know what he's trying to do. He's trying to get me upset. But because I know what he's doing, I'm going to think about what my job is and not let him ruin my game.' "

"That sounds good, coach," Jerome said. "I hope I can remember that during a game."

"You won't be perfect at it," the coach said, "but remind your-self of it during the game, and practice using it. You'll get better at it. In fact, I'll write down the steps so you'll be able to remember them, okay? You can put them up in your locker."

"Okay, coach," Jerome said, "thanks a lot."

Teens who should learn this approach for managing their anger are the Denier, the Clam, the Confronter (who in many situations—such as a game—can't confront), and the Rocket.

8. Exercise and Physical Activity

What happens when people get angry? Their blood pressure goes up. But exercise lowers the blood pressure. Regular exercise pro-motes good health because it not only lowers blood pressure, it also reduces depression and lowers cholesterol. And it helps kids blow off steam in a constructive way.

And what about stress? Exercise helps to relieve tension and stress. If you have a teenager who gets too little exercise, the chances are that he has fewer ways to work out those feelings. Teens who exercise regularly and vigorously can experience a dramatic drop in tension, stress, and anxiety.

And it doesn't take that much exercise. Recent research sug-gests that just 20 minutes of vigorous aerobic exercise (such as fast walking, jogging, swimming, or bicycling) reduces tension. The effects last up to three hours.

And why does exercise work? It may be that it distracts

kids from their troubles. It also may be because of the effect on the brain—a vigorous workout sparks the production of endorphins, the body chemicals that promote a sense of well-being. Plus, exercise raises your body temperature, which may trigger changes in other brain chemicals that help ease anxiety.

Encourage your teen to get moving and to get active. Develop an exercise or fitness program together. Adolescents, often concerned about the appearance of their bodies, are frequently interested in weight lifting, jogging, or playing a sport with a parent because of the advantages to their bodies.

That can be the hook, but if they also have problems with anger, then getting them involved in regular, consistent, vigorous exercise should help them to be better able to cope with anger, stress, and frustration. The Avenger and The Rocket would benefit from exercise in controlling their anger.

9. Changing Negative Feelings into Positive Action

You can be sure that in working with adolescents I have used lots of real-life situations that will get them involved and help them understand what I'm teaching. One of those situations is the one involving the National Basketball Association player Latrell Sprewell.

Sprewell, a star player on the Golden State Warriors, got mad at his coach, P.J. Carlesimo, during practice one day in the 1997–1998 season and attacked the coach. He grabbed him by the throat, reports have stated, and then after leaving the gym came back and physically attacked him once more.

That incident led to Sprewell being suspended by the team and then by the NBA. In addition, he reportedly lost major endorsements and forfeited his salary. All told, he lost several million dollars and was not able to play for the remainder of the season.

Many, if not most, of the teens I work with have heard of the Sprewell incident. And most teens seem to feel sympathetic toward Sprewell. They say that if his coach hadn't ridden Sprewell so hard or hadn't used name-calling or whatever he did, Sprewell wouldn't have attacked him. Under the circumstances, they say, Sprewell had every right to attack him.

"I won't argue that with you on moral grounds," I say. "But let's look at what it cost Sprewell to blow up and act out his anger. Was it worth it to lose several million dollars and not be able to play the game he loves?"

They have to reluctantly admit that it was not worth it—he lost a lot.

Then I ask, "Did he have to physically attack his coach?"

"Yeah," teens will say, "what was he going to do, let the coach treat him bad?"

"If he wanted to keep playing basketball, the game he loved, and if he wanted to keep earning his millions of dollars in salary and endorsements, could he have handled it in a different way?"

That's a bit difficult for tough adolescents. They don't like to back down. But on the other hand, they can admit there were options.

"Okay," I ask, "tell me some of his options. What if the coach was dead wrong in what he did? What if the coach deserved to be fired for what he did?"

"Well, he could have told on him," someone will venture.

"That's right," I'll say. "Let's face it, in the NBA, players more or less run teams. He could have gone to the general manager or the president of the team and demanded that Carlesimo be reprimanded because he was damaging team morale. Other players have done that and survived.

"What else could he have done?" I ask.

"He could have talked to sports writers," someone else says.

"True," I'll say. "The press has a lot of power in sports, and Sprewell could have gotten his story out by talking about the coach's tactics. But what about just being assertive? Without physically attacking him, he could have confronted the coach in an assertive way and let him know that his behavior was inappropriate.

"Now," I'll tell them, "you have the idea about what taking negative feelings and turning them into positive action is all about. Sprewell had choices. Because he acted impulsively, he chose a course of action that cost him a lot. He lost out in money, in time, and in what people thought about him. His anger and his attack on the coach wasn't worth it. Sprewell couldn't play during his suspension, but the coach is still coaching.

"You can take your anger and plan a course of action that doesn't cost you and that lets you work out the problem in your own way so you don't lose out."

And I go on to say that there are other situations in which people can turn negatives into positives. I tell adolescents about my high school experiences with an algebra teacher. I didn't like this teacher, and I don't think he liked me. I thought he wasn't teaching me very well, and I got so mad one day that I walked out of the class and went to see my guidance counselor. She reminded me that I needed this class to graduate and that I couldn't change classes or teachers midsemester. I had to go back to the class.

I went back, but instead of taking it out on him or me, I decided—actually vowed to myself—that I would get through his class and that when I went to college I would show this teacher that I could excel at math. One day, I told myself, I will bring a report card from college and show him good grades in algebra and math.

Did I ever do that? No. But I kept my promise to myself. I got As and Bs in every algebra and statistics course I took in undergraduate and graduate school. I even went on to teach statistics in a college. I guess I showed him!

Okay, so he never knew. That didn't matter because I had turned a negative situation into a positive, and I had the satisfaction of knowing (or at least thinking) that there was nothing wrong with me as a student—he was just a poor teacher.

Changing the negative emotion of anger into positive action would appeal to the Denier and to the Clam; it could also be helpful to the Crab, the Rocket, and the Avenger.

GOLDEN OPPORTUNITIES TO TEACH ABOUT ANGER MANAGEMENT

The best golden opportunities to teach about anger come about because of a crisis brought on by a teen's anger—your own or someone else's.

Earlier in this chapter I told about Phil, who got charged with resisting arrest after an argument with his girlfriend. Well, after spending a night in jail, he felt ashamed and guilty for what he put his girlfriend, his parents, and himself through. After he got home, he and his parents talked about his problems with his temper. It was at that time—perhaps the lowest point in his life—that Phil could admit that he had a problem with his anger and that he needed to do something about it.

As with many teens who have an anger-control problem, it took a crisis for Phil to look more critically and insightfully at himself and to admit that he needed to make some changes. Whether the crisis is breaking a valued object, hurting another person, getting suspended from school, causing a breakup with a girlfriend, or losing a job, it can precipitate looking inward.

When 17-year-old Matt shoved his mother during an argument, he was shaken by his own behavior. "I've never hurt my mother before," he said. "I don't know what came over me, but I was just so angry at her." He apologized several times to his mother, and she used the occasion to talk about some of the problems between them as well as about his anger for the first time in several years.

He was ready to agree he had to do something to learn to calm down when he got angry.

Jessie's parents had a golden opportunity to discuss their son's anger after he got fired from his job. Jessie, at 16, was working for a landscape company. It was hard, dirty work, but he enjoyed both the work and the money he was now bringing in. But one day at work, Jessie's boss thought he was being too careless with some expensive shrubs they were planting. In reprimanding him, his boss implied Jessie was stupid. Jessie blew up and yelled obscenities at his boss. He was immediately fired.

It was embarrassing for Jessie to come home and admit what he'd done to lose a job he liked so much. His parents, presented with a golden opportunity, waited for a couple of hours before talking to him.

"Was what your boss said so bad?" his mother asked.

"Yeah, it was," Jessie replied.

"Bad enough to lose a job you really liked?" his father asked.

"No, I guess not," said Jessie. "I didn't want to stop working there."

"It seems like your anger got you in trouble," his mother said gently.

"I know," Jessie said. "I shouldn't have said those things to him."

"You might be able to get your job back if you apologize," his father offered. "But more importantly, maybe you need to learn some ways to keep your anger under control so this doesn't happen again."

"I know," said Jessie. "I've tried to control my anger, but I'm not very good at it."

"We noticed that," his mother said smiling. "But there's a couple of things we do to keep our anger under control. If you want, maybe we could teach them to you. Then you won't have to lose a job that you really like again. Okay?"

"Yeah," Jessie said. "I guess you better show me."

PUTTING IT INTO ACTION

Because it is important that teenagers have an overall knowledge of anger and how to deal with it, you will need to teach the activities in the five areas that follow.

1. Discuss the key concepts about anger with your adolescent. The key concepts are these:

- Anger is powerful, but it doesn't have to make you lose control.
- Displaced anger is taking out your anger on someone else.
- Ignoring your anger can cause it to become stronger or to come out in different ways.
- Telling people what they did to make you mad can lead to feelings of empowerment.
- Many people often feel powerless when they're mad at situations over which they have no control and have no hope of changing.
- There are several important and effective techniques to help you manage your anger.
- Channeling is a way of dealing with anger that involves turning negative emotion into positive action.

2. Teach your teen the three-step anger-management method:

- Learn to identify his or her anger triggers.
- Learn to identify his or her anger style.
- Learn several anger-management techniques.

3. Teach your teens to identify their anger triggers.

- Teach them what anger triggers are, and have them identify and name the most important things that trigger their anger.

- Have them record their anger triggers for a week to gain understanding of what gets them angry.

- Teach them that knowing their triggers helps them to know under what circumstances they need to use anger-management techniques.

4. Teach your teens to identify anger styles.

    - Teach them about different anger styles and how to identify their predominant anger style.

    - Ask them to track their anger styles by recording the way they react during a typical week.

    - Teach them that knowing their typical anger style means they can watch for it and work at changing to one that works better for them.

5. Teach your teen to use one or more of the major anger-management techniques as based on their particular anger style:

    - Confront the other person in an assertive way.

    - Use a breathing technique to relax.

    - Use progressive relaxation.

    - Use autogenic training.

    - Use a visualization approach.

    - Listen to soothing music.

    - Use a thinking approach: Stop and Think.

    - Exercise and be physically active.

    - Change negative feelings into positive action.

7

STEP SIX: TEACH YOUR TEENAGER TO RESOLVE CONFLICTS PEACEFULLY

When I begin talking about and teaching methods of nonviolent conflict resolution in group sessions with teenagers, the responses from the kids are swift and judgmental:

"Man, that's not the way it is out on the street."
"Maybe that's the way the Brady Bunch solves problems, but we got our own ways!"
"That's so fake, man. That's not the way anybody settles problems."

From their point of view, they're right. In their circumscribed world, everyone settles conflicts and problems with loud words, fists, and guns. They've grown up to believe that if you don't handle things in a tough way, you'll end up a loser. And once you back down from someone who is threatening a fight, you'll be labeled a wimp or a punk from then on. Even worse, avoid a fight and you'll have vultures taking advantage of you. That's the way things work in many of the schools, neighborhoods, and troubled families where tough, hardened teenagers live.

A few years ago, I was asked by a local affiliate of a network television station to come on the five o'clock news and comment on a breaking news story. I had heard about this situation before I got to the station. A mother and a father had been arrested and charged with child abuse for forcing their children to fight each other. Before I went on the air, I was given a chance to see a video that had been "produced" by these parents.

The video was homemade and taken by the parents when they forced their six-year-old twins (one girl and one boy) to fight with each other in an effort to settle problems of sibling fighting! In the video, the children were encouraged by their parents to hit, kick, knee, pummel, pound, and hurt each other as much as possible. The children were crying and wanted to stop, but the parents wouldn't let them. At the end of the 11-minute video, the boy had a bloody face, and both children were bruised and disheveled.

The intent, the parents argued in their own behalf, was to teach the children that fighting was unpleasant and that they should avoid it and get along better. Many parents would agree this is obviously not the way to teach this lesson to children. Yet, in less dramatic and somewhat more indirect ways, many parents in fact do train their children in just such an irrational fashion.

When we parents do not solve our own problems and conflicts with kindness, sensitivity, and verbal means, we are modeling and exhibiting a how-to course for our children. Especially in a family where there is domestic violence, parents have unintentionally designed their own conflict-resolution training course that teaches children to be violent and aggressive.

Shawna, a 14-year-old girl in one of my therapy groups, had been hit frequently by her mother for being disobedient when she was a child. After living with her mother until age 11, she went to live with her father. Shawna was exposed to more violence there because when she sneaked out of the house or didn't come home on time, her father slapped or punched her. One day Shawna came to group therapy and complained about having a sore arm and pains in her chest. She also showed us blood on her leg where she had been kicked. She had told us previously about being hit with a chair. There was no wondering, as far as I was concerned, as to why Shawna got into fights and overreacted when there was a conflict with other teenagers. She had never been taught how to resolve problems in peaceful, nonaggressive ways.

TEACHING CONFLICT RESOLUTION

The problem with teaching appropriate conflict resolution tactics is that you may not know instinctively how best to teach your teen strategies to peacefully resolve and settle arguments, disagreements, conflicts, and problems. For instance, you might have mixed feelings about how best to advise your child if she has to confront a bully at school.

Many parents, perhaps most parents, believe children need to stand up to and fight any bully who threatens them. If you believe this, then even if you want to teach your child to be nonviolent, you may not be sure what to teach. Adding to your confusion or your mixed feelings are the ways disagreements and conflicts are actually dealt with in your family.

Thirteen-year-old Ryan was described by his parents as belligerent and argumentative. It turned out that discussions and minor disagreements between the parents often got out of control. In one such argument, which both parents later agreed was petty, Ryan's parents disagreed over the pruning of a tree in the yard. Ryan's father wanted to trim the tree because he thought it was too bushy and overgrown. Ryan's mother wanted it left alone because she liked the leafy look and the shade the tree provided. However, while she was shopping one day, the father pruned the tree. As soon as the mother saw the results, she exploded at her husband for trimming the tree when he knew she disagreed.

As the argument developed, the couple traded insults and brought in other issues. At one point, Ryan's father said he was "sick and tired" of trying to live with a woman who didn't appreciate him and he would move out and get a divorce. When Ryan overheard this argument, he ran into the kitchen where the fight was going on and got between his parents, imploring them not to fight. Ryan's intervention helped to de-escalate the fight, but not before his mother slammed cupboard doors and his father broke a dish.

When the family talked about this argument with Ryan's psychologist, Ryan said he was most bothered by his parents mentioning a divorce.

"You know we didn't mean that," his father said.

"We weren't that mad," his mother agreed, echoing her husband.

But it was clear that his parents' fight weighed heavily on Ryan's mind and that he truly was afraid they would get a divorce. While the couple had made up and gotten over the fight within hours, Ryan could only think of the bitter and resentful words he had heard, which he believed would bring about a divorce. How did he know that they had made up and that they really weren't that mad?

Ryan's parents had a golden opportunity to teach Ryan how to argue constructively and to resolve problems in a peaceful and productive way. They missed out on this opportunity, and only later did they understand the full impact this kind of destructive fight had on their son. In effect, they had a chance to take a legitimate issue (a conflict over pruning a tree) and resolve it in a win-win manner.

Ryan's parents, recognizing they had a difference of opinion about the pruning of the tree, could have discussed their opinions openly and tried to seek a compromise. With some discussion and brainstorming of ideas, they very likely could have found a solution both of them found acceptable.

After that conflict, no matter what they preached to Ryan about the best ways to handle problems and conflicts, Ryan was being trained by what he witnessed. Like children and teens in other families, Ryan needs to learn at home how to handle conflicts so that both sides win. Watching appropriate and peaceful conflict resolution, while given techniques for dealing with conflicts, would best teach him how to settle his own problems constructively.

HEALTHY CONFLICT RESOLUTION

Resolving conflicts in appropriate, peaceful ways requires that adolescents learn about healthy communication styles, which include "I" messages and assertiveness, brainstorming, negotiation, and finding win-win solutions.

In daily family life, which involves conflicts over such real-life issues as dealing with bullies, sibling fighting, and pruning the tree in the yard, you will have many opportunities to model healthy and appropriate conflict resolution. When you take advantage of these golden opportunities, you will literally have hundreds of chances over the years to show your children how to solve sticky situations. If you usually deal with such situations with hostility, aggression, and violence, you will teach your teens to be hostile, aggressive, and violent themselves. If you use non-violent ways, you will teach nonviolence.

I remember an occasion when I was president of a fairly large neighborhood association. One Sunday afternoon I got a call from one of our neighbors, reporting that there were some drunken bullies from outside the neighborhood who had invaded the small beach area near the lake adjoining the neighborhood. They were creating a nuisance, and many neighbors with children were not able to enjoy themselves. The kicker from the caller was: "Since you're the president, would you go down to the beach and take care of this?"

I'm rather small of stature, and anyone who knows me would confirm that I'm anything but tough. So, I took a deep breath, pulled up my five-foot-nine-inch, 155-pound frame, and went off to the beach to do battle with Hell's Angels. My daughter Jill, who was fairly young, asked to go, but I suggested she stay home with her mom. I walked the two blocks to the beach, hoping, of course, that by the time I got there the troublemakers would be gone.

But, no, they were still there. They didn't look so bad, but they were a bunch of young men in their twenties running around with beer cans and taking frisbees away from little kids and generally having a good time—albeit a drunken good time at the expense of others.

I walked slowly into the park and went up to the first guy I saw.

"Hi," I said quietly. "What's happening down here today?"

"Not much, man, want a beer?" the young man asked.

"No, thanks," I replied. "Seems like we got a problem." I hooked my hands in the back pockets of my jeans. Although I didn't look threatening, I wanted to appear even less of a threat.

"Yeah, what's that?" the young man asked belligerently.

"I'm getting calls from people saying that there are some rowdies down here. You seen anything like that?"

"Naw," the man said. "We're not bothering anyone."

"I can see that," I said. "I wonder what we can do so nobody's calling me?"

"We'll be good," he said. "We just came in for a swim and to have a good time."

"Yep, I can see that, " I replied. "We have a nice park and beach area, don't you think?"

"Yeah, it's nice," he agreed.

"Will you do me a favor?" I asked.

"What's that?" he asked.

"Have fun and stay away from the children and families who are enjoying their Sunday afternoon here. Then you'll be able to come back and enjoy the beach another day."

"No problem, man," he said. "We'll just do our own thing."

"You're welcome to do that," I said, "and I would really appreciate you helping me out like this. Have a nice afternoon."

I turned away and walked over to a picnic table and sat

down. I watched things for a while, waved at a few neighbors, and hoped that the visitors wouldn't start any more trouble. The young man I had talked to went over to his friends, and I could hear one of them ask him if they had been kicked out. The young man said no, I was a nice guy, and they could stay but they had to leave the little kids alone. The rest shook their heads and went into the water.

In less than an hour, they headed out of the park to their car and took off. I went home and told my family what had happened. Even though my daughter Jill wasn't at the park, she heard about that encounter not just once but a few times as we had to repeat it for several neighbors who had heard about the incident and wanted to know how it ended. For Jill, it was a lesson in one way to resolve a problem. The situation could have resulted in a hostile interaction, but that's not what I wanted. At the time I wasn't thinking about the incident as a golden opportunity to teach Jill about conflict resolution. Afterward, I realized that in an indirect way that's exactly what it was.

Healthy conflict resolution involves:

- Addressing conflict in peaceful ways
- Efforts to find areas of agreement
- Compromise
- A settlement that allows everyone to save face

SEVEN QUICK RESOLUTION TOOLS FOR MINOR CONFLICTS

How can you teach healthy conflict resolution to your teenager? I'm going to answer this question in the next several pages in a systematic way. First, I'll start by giving seven quick tools you can teach (and use) when there's a *minor* conflict or problem.

1. Flip a Coin

One objective way to handle a minor, two-sided problem is to flip a coin. Of course, both parties have to agree that the outcome of the coin flip will direct their actions. For instance, if two children want to watch different TV programs at the same time, an easy way to resolve the problem is to suggest that they let a flip of a coin determine which program they watch. This tool can govern lots of situations for children, from who sits in the front seat of the car to who gets to choose the movie the family will watch.

2. Split the Difference

A second way of dealing with a conflict is to split the difference. What this means is that two people, instead of trying to determine an absolute winner, agree to compromise. In a compromise, there is a more or less equitable way both parties get part of what they want. For example, if Ryan's parents had thought of this quick tool for conflict resolution and used it, they might have found a solution in which dad could have trimmed some of the tree, but not so much that mom couldn't live with it. Other situations in which splitting the difference can provide a workable solution include those where two children wish to use a video game or two people want to use a computer exclusively for a certain length of time. Instead they agree to split the time.

3. Skip It

The "skip it" solution is a very useful tool for all of us at times. It's certainly a good one to teach teens. When you use "skip it" as a quick conflict resolution tool, you give up a fight because you decide it isn't worth the time, effort, and energy. Some things are worth fighting about, others aren't. Of course, what's worth fighting or arguing about is different for all of us, but at least we can teach our kids that they can learn to recognize which are which for them—learn to choose their battles. When children complain that certain things aren't fair, often they are right. But is it always worth making a big deal about?

A teenager told me that a tough boy who belonged to a local gang had embarrassed him at school in front of his friends. He wanted to get even. I asked him what would happen if he tried to get even. "I might get shot by someone in the gang," he replied.

"Is it worth getting killed over?" I asked.

"I was really dissed," he said.

"I know that, and I know being put down in front of friends makes us really mad," I said. "But is it worth getting killed over? Are you willing to lose your life over an embarrassment?"

Some things are more important than an embarrassment. For instance, a close relationship or a job. Ruth, a woman I know, applied for a job opening in the company where she had worked for several years. Getting the position would have meant a promotion and an increase in salary. After interviewing for the position, the job was given to another person who had worked for the company for a very short period of time.

Ruth was angry and hurt that she had been passed over. "I wasn't even given a chance to prove that I could do the job," she said. She considered resigning from the company and she thought about angrily confronting her boss, who had made the decision to hire the other person.

"I decided," Ruth said later, "that it wasn't in my best interest to either quit my job or confront the boss. If I quit my job, I wouldn't have any job. And if I confronted my boss, I might end up with a worse relationship with him."

She decided her best course of action was to skip it. "My best bet," Ruth said, "was to drop my anger and move on, continuing to do the best job I could in my present position."

Ruth's decision to skip it proved to be a wise one because she needed a recommendation from her boss a few months later for an even better position that opened up within the company.

4. Say You're Sorry

There's nothing so truly magical for cooling down a potentially explosive situation than to say, "I'm sorry." It takes guts and humility, but it works very well. When a person who is mad at you hears the words "I'm sorry," anger usually melts away. Most of us have made lots of mistakes in life—often angering others in the process. Anyone who's married knows what I'm talking about. You can't always explain adequately why you've done something stupid or unthinking, and attempting to justify your actions just won't do it. However, a sincere "I'm sorry" can turn a losing conflict into a chance to find a solution for the future.

In raising my own children, one of the things I have tried to teach them is to take responsibility for their mistakes or errors and apologize. Now, it's true that when a child does something deliberate to another child and we demand they say they're sorry, they aren't going to feel remorse or guilt. But the words "I'm sorry" help soothe the other person's upset and can de-escalate a hot situation.

I'm not suggesting that children be taught to use these words to heal every situation or to avoid taking responsibility for their actions, but they can cool down someone else's anger. Often "I'm sorry" can be followed by an admission of responsibility. For instance, an adolescent boy who was hanging out with his buddies and failed to call his girlfriend when he said he would can never adequately explain not picking up the phone and giving a call. However, if he says, "I'm sorry, I should have called when I said I would. I was wrong," he will have helped defuse her anger, and they can talk about avoiding this problem in the future. By excusing himself or placing the blame on others he will only intensify his girlfriend's anger.

Parents can find many golden opportunities in the course of family life to demonstrate how to use "I'm sorry." I remember once having my two children in the car along with several of their friends during a trip to visit a nursing home. I was speeding and not paying enough attention to how fast I was going. A policeman pulled me over.

I could have said, "How dare you pull me over! Can't you see I have six kids in the car and we're on a mission of mercy! You have no right to give me a ticket!" But that would only have caused a greater problem (who knows how sympathetic or bullying the officer might be?) and would have certainly led to my making excuses (the kids were distracting me; I was lost; I was trying to find this nursing home; etc.). What I would have taught the children was that I don't accept responsibility for problems and I invite conflict.

What I said was: "I'm sorry, sir, I think I was going too fast for this road."

"Yes, sir," he replied, "you were. I'd like you to keep your speed down in this stretch of road. You've got some valuable cargo there."

"Yes, sir. Thanks for reminding me."

I avoided a ticket, sure, but more importantly I taught all of the kids in the car that day something important. Taking responsibility for one's actions and apologizing is sometimes the way to go because it can quickly defuse the annoyance or anger of another person.

5. Laugh It Off

A funny response, a joking reply, or a bit of humor can rescue many a situation, particularly one that threatens to get out of hand. Children and teenagers often react defensively—usually because they are not yet secure enough to laugh at themselves or to allow anyone else to laugh at them—and they have difficulty with this quick way to resolve a potential problem. But it is a good idea to teach our children to use this conflict resolution technique because it can save young people from fights and hostility.

When I was growing up, I wasn't much of a fighter. I had to develop a sense of humor. Turning the humor at myself or just making light of a situation helped me over and over again as I went through school. When the teenagers I now work with ask me to tell them about my last fight, they are incredulous and amazed when I tell them I was in the fourth grade when a friendly wrestling match with a friend got out of hand. They think there is something strange about someone who hasn't had a fist fight in almost fifty years!

But what I want to teach them is that they could live the same way by using humor and laughter once in a while. In group and individual therapy with young people, I try to teach them how to use humor to cool off situations. A quick wit and a ready laugh will defuse someone else's attempt to start a fight.

As always, the teaching works best if you can model it and also model the security that goes with it. In the D'Souza family, Pam D'Souza, a psychologist, developed a unique and humorous way to remind both her sons, Ben and Bryan, as well as her husband, Mario, to laugh off situations. Pam invented Victorious Duck.

Victorious Duck is a fictitious character who lets things roll off his back, like water rolls off the back of real ducks. If a member of the family allows a hurt, an offense, or a conflict to slide off his or her back, they get a point on the Victorious Duck Chart. The person with the most points at the end of the week becomes Victorious Duck for the week and receives a special prize as well.

Recently, Pam noted that Mario checked out the chart and saw that he had fewer points than his sons. "When he found he was losing," Pam recalls, "he tried harder to let more situations slide off his back." And, she adds, "When any one of us thinks of Victorious Duck, we can't help but chuckle."

A Victorious Duck can help you keep situations in perspective and help you and your family laugh off some of the less important issues. When the issues or conflicts are really important, then they should be handled in more direct or assertive ways.

6. Walk Away

Like the "skip it" approach, this quick conflict resolution technique involves just dropping the subject. It differs from "skip it" in that here you actually leave the situation. And, not surprisingly, walking away could be the best way of avoiding a physical confrontation. One of the things our children need to learn is that no one can make them fight. Many aggressive young people actually say they *had* to fight or they *couldn't* back down. From their perspective, it is next to impossible to walk away from someone who wants a physical conflict. Many young people believe that others will think less of them if they walk away. When you practice "walking away" in your family, it will be easier for your child to do the same.

Mary practices this in her family because she found that it often works well in her marriage to her husband Mike. Having done it in front of her children, Paige and Broc, she says that it's a good way to teach them to do the same. She recalls a time recently when the method had to be employed with the children present.

"Mike bought a couch for the den in our new house," Mary recalls. "I had my heart set on an entertainment center for the room and he found this big leather couch that he bought without consulting me.

"When he told me one evening that the couch was going to be delivered the next day, I was furious that he hadn't consulted me. I told him how I felt and what I had wanted to do. He said that he lives here, too, and he had a right to buy furniture. Although I wanted to continue the argument because I was so mad, I knew it wasn't the right time or place.

" 'I'm not arguing about this now,' I said to Mike, and I left the room. Later, after the children were asleep, we started talking about it, got some things off our chests, and settled it."

By walking away at first, it changed the dynamics of a conflict that could have led to a big fight. Later, after both Mary and

Mike had cooled down, they discussed it and reached an agreement that suited both of them. While the children didn't get to hear the actual settlement, they would in the days that followed see how their parents had resolved it and how they acted toward each other. Your teens need to understand that walking away doesn't mean the problem won't be addressed, just that it will be resolved at a later time.

7. Be Agreeable

You can teach your children one last quick solution to relatively uncomplicated conflicts—to be agreeable. When someone has a problem with you, the last thing they want, if they're determined to fight, is for you to agree with them. They'd prefer that you be disagreeable. This allows them to justify their stance and to be mean with impunity.

Just saying "I agree" helps to undercut a lot of anger and hostility. I know that when I've had people mad at me, saying that I agree with some part of what their beef is helps. Admitting that I acted in some way that was reprehensible or wrong takes some of the wind out of their sails. After they're prepared to tell me all the ways I was wrong and betrayed them or hurt them, having me agree throws them. They usually aren't prepared for agreement.

It helps if you are sincere and that your admission of responsibility is said in a sincere, straightforward manner.

For example, Judy and her family were spending a summer day at the lake using their motor boat to water ski. After several hours, two men in a small boat came up to them and very unkindly yelled that they were going way too fast.

"The water is high because of flooding, and there's a law that you can't go over six miles an hour," one of the men yelled.

Neither Judy nor her husband had heard about this and Judy

said as sweetly as possible, "Thank you for letting us know we were going too fast."

That didn't stop the men from continuing to yell, but Judy repeated, "Thank you so much for letting us know we were doing something wrong. We'll stop now."

The men began to calm down, explained more about the high lake level, and went away.

In this situation, as in others in which this technique can work, once there is that first agreement ("Thank you for telling us we were doing something wrong"), the two sides can look for other ways to agree and for ways to fix the initial problem. And that's what conflict resolution is all about.

SOLVING MORE COMPLICATED CONFLICTS

More complicated and complex conflicts require more work and aren't as likely to be quickly settled. That's when you'll need to teach your children to bring out the more complicated and advanced strategies for conflict resolution.

Appropriate Communication

These strategies all have to do with appropriate communication. Teaching your teen a few simple (but often hard to apply) communication skills can settle many a difficult problem.

Let's take a look at one girl's conflict as an example. Sixteen-year-old Chantel told me that she heard that another girl at school, Heather, was after Chantel's boyfriend. As soon as Chantel heard this, she was fighting mad. She was ready to wait at Heather's bus stop, grab her, and slam her into the side of the bus.

Chantel was ready to act on hearsay information. If she had

done this, she might have been arrested and charged with assault. But what did she really know about the situation? All she knew was what she had heard.

What Chantel needed to do in this situation was to get some facts. But she couldn't do this by grabbing someone and throwing her down or socking her. The only way to get the facts is to talk to the other person. In order to talk, to communicate, effectively in such a situation, young people have to learn four essential aspects of this kind of communication:

1. Stay calm.

2. Don't accuse or blame.

3. Ask questions to get information.

4. Listen to the other person's explanation.

If Chantel is going to get the facts, she will have to approach Heather, preferably when they can talk alone. But first, Chantel has to be calm. She can't be fighting mad. It's better, therefore, that she wait to get her initial anger under control. Having done this, she may look for an opportunity to confront Heather.

The confrontation is not going to work, though, if Chantel starts out with accusations and blame. If she begins with a statement like, "Yo, bitch, I heard you're after my boyfriend. I always knew you were a lowdown, dirty scumbag of a loser," the only thing that's likely to happen is that Heather may start calling her names or swinging at Chantel's nose.

But staying calm and asking some questions will help Chantel get some facts about the situation. Chantel needs to clarify what's going on and this will require beginning in a way that is less likely to start an immediate fight. For instance, Chantel could say, "Heather, I've been hearing things I'd like to talk about" or "Heather, can we talk for a minute?" She can follow this up with, "Can I ask you about something I heard?"

Even if Heather is hostile, this approach is not likely to make her more hostile or to provoke a physical fight. Heather might be skeptical or wary, but Chantel's questions are not likely to start a war.

Chantel has to ask questions in a nonthreatening way, and she has to be ready to listen to the answers. If Chantel comes out and says, "I heard you were interested in my boyfriend, is this true?" and follows this up with nonthreatening questions and acts in a nonbelligerent manner, no matter what Heather's attitude, a fight is unlikely to follow. Often when kids really hear an explanation, there is no basis for a fight.

Another approach is to go to her boyfriend and ask him if he is interested in Heather. That could clear the problem up quickly if Chantel asks him questions in a calm manner.

However, even if we assume the worst possible scenario with a hostile and aggressive Heather who says, "Yeah, I like your boyfriend and I'm going to take him from you!" a calm Chantel can comment on this. She could say, "Thanks for being honest with me, but I have no intention of letting him go. Good luck to you!"

In the end, Chantel may be relieved to hear Heather's explanation, or she may be threatened by the girl's position. However, either way she has more information than she had before, and she can be respectful of Heather without getting into a fight.

Body Language

One key aspect of this approach is body language. Young people need to learn early in life that they convey messages with their body just as much as they do with their words. What people feel is often indicated by the positions of their hands and arms, the way their eyebrows are arched, or the way they are standing.

Body language is an aspect of communication that you can

practice and role-play with your teens. Are they standing in a way that conveys interest or disinterest? Are their hands balled up into a fist suggesting that they are ready to fight? Are their arms folded in a defensive manner? Or do they have their arms skeptically placed on their hips? Are they looking the other person in the eye or glancing at the floor? You can show your teen what her body is communicating by asking her to stand in front of a mirror to see for herself. This level of awareness can pay off in important conversations or confrontations.

Tone of Voice

Teaching your teen to be aware of and to use his tone of voice in the most effective way can also help him make sure the message he is sending is the one being heard.

Having your teen listen to a tape recording of his voice while practicing some of these conflict resolution techniques can be valuable. Often teens talk in ways that sound meaner or tougher than they actually intend. When they are trying to resolve a conflict without violence, they must make sure their voice conveys kindness rather than gruffness.

Getting Unstuck

Too often, I find, when young people are involved in a conflict, they get stuck in that conflict. For many children and teens, it is very difficult to move from this stuck position to an unstuck position—one that allows for the resolution of the problem or conflict. Here's an example of a conflict that is stuck in a rut:

PARENT: "Every time you go out, you come home late!"

TEEN: "That's not true! You never remember all the times I come home early or on time."

PARENT: "That's because there aren't any. I just can't trust you to keep your curfew."

TEEN: "Well, it's too early anyway. No one else has to come in at ten o'clock at night. If I got to stay out later, I could come in on time."

PARENT: "How could I give you a later curfew when you're not responsible enough to come in on time now?"

This argument is going nowhere fast. It is, in a word, stuck. At least three things contribute to people getting and staying stuck in an argument or fight:

- An inability to listen to the other person
- An inability to express real needs in an effective way
- An inability to use communication that moves an argument or disagreement along

It's a given that listening to the other person is essential in any effective communication. And, along with staying calm, listening might be the most important thing in a conflict situation. But people also have to ask each other questions to clarify situations and needs.

The problem when people get stuck is that they are stating their own position—often without telling the other person what their real needs are. Getting unstuck requires that each person go beyond talking about what he or she thinks and how awful the other person is. It means listening to what the other person needs and repeating it out loud. We all have needs—a feeling or an emotion—in conflicts, otherwise there wouldn't be conflicts. However, most of us *don't* start out by saying what our real need is. Usually we disguise it.

Using "I" Messages

When my son was away at college and he hadn't called in two or three weeks, I called him up and told him I hadn't heard from him lately. The discussion that followed revolved around his saying he was busy with classes and work and my responding that he seemed to have time to do everything else but call us. Now, if we were both honest about our needs and feelings, we would use "I" messages and say things like:

ME: "I worry about you when I don't hear from you every week. I sometimes imagine that something has happened to you."
JASON: "I want to feel that I am grown up and self-reliant and that I don't have to call my parents all the time."

If we both said things like this, it would help us to know what was really going on with each other, and we would be clear about the issues involved. It's not about phone calls and being busy, it's about worried parents and a son trying to grow up and away from his parents. Having gotten this far, our conflict would be a lot simpler to solve. It's not impossible to solve an argument about him being too busy and about me being mad because he doesn't call enough, but it sure is a waste of time and energy given the real needs we have.

The trick is to get beyond these outward messages and positions and start talking about what we really feel. But how do people do that?

Argument Transformers

One tool I find effective with teens is what I call "argument transformers." These are questions or comments that move a stuck argument from stop to go. Keep in mind that these argument transformers are for older children and adolescents, not young children. Here are a few of these argument transformers:

"This isn't really about me being late is it?"
"You seem to be angrier (or some other feeling) than the situation warrants."
"Can we talk about your feelings?"
"What do you really need from me?"
"I think you're so mad (or some other feeling) because . . ."

The use of an argument transformer can help two people begin to talk about the real issues underlying a conflict. When the real emotions are brought to the surface, then the argument can center on them, and both parties can acknowledge what each other is feeling:

ME: "I didn't know you felt that calling us made you feel too dependent on us."
JASON: "I didn't think you worried about me anymore."

Then, a different kind of transformer has to be used. Basically, this kind of transformer will be expressed like this: "How are we going to solve this?" No matter what the conflict, once people have stated and acknowledged each other's needs, then there has to be discussion of how the problem is going to be settled in a peaceful way.

Win-Win Solutions

Because real needs and feelings have been expressed and acknowledged, a good solution will be one that takes the feelings and needs of each side into account—this is a win-win solution.

There are four steps to reaching a win-win solution:

1. Brainstorming for solutions
2. Negotiating
3. Compromising
4. Selecting the best solution for both sides

In teaching teens about this part of conflict resolution, you have to know how to brainstorm solutions and to end up with a workable one that meets the needs of both sides, at least to some extent. That's what we call compromise. But compromise is sometimes difficult. That's why children need models and examples of compromise as well as brainstorming, negotiation, and picking a win-win solution.

David Cochran's mother had a problem with David—well, not really with 14-year-old David, but with the jersey number he selected when he made the ninth-grade basketball team. He selected the number thirteen. Mrs. Cochran was superstitious, worried a lot about her only child, and was frightened that his selection of that number thirteen was a bad omen. When she brought this up to David, he thought her fears were silly, and he said he would not go to the basketball coach and ask for a new number.

"Why not?" his mother asked.

"Because," David told her, "that would mean taking someone else's number and I would have to explain that I have a psycho for a mother."

"That's not fair," Mrs. Cochran replied, "but I can see that would be difficult for you."

David wanted to continue the discussion and turn it into an argument that would go nowhere: "I don't see why you're so worried about the number thirteen. There are professional players who wear it and nothing happens to them."

"I know you don't understand this," she said, "but it's just the way I feel and I want you to wear another number. Let's see what we can do about it."

"Well, I won't talk to the coach," David said.

"I could talk to the coach," his mother suggested.

"You could talk to him before school when no one is around his office," countered David, offering his own suggestion.

"How about if I go first thing tomorrow before school and make sure no other kids are there?"

"Only if you don't talk about your stupid superstitions," David said.

"I'll do my best about that," his mother said.

"And don't embarrass me," David said.

"I'll try," his mother agreed.

The next morning she went to the school, found the coach alone in his office, and presented the situation to him. He was very understanding and agreed to locate another jersey and number for David. The problem was solved. David was quietly given the new jersey and it was not brought up in front of the team.

In this situation, with his mother's reasonable and calm responses as a guide, she and David brainstormed the situation and compromised on a solution. In the process she taught him that a compromise can work out with each person feeling comfortable about the end result.

GOLDEN OPPORTUNITIES TO TEACH ABOUT PEACEFUL CONFLICT RESOLUTION

Family life provides plenty of golden opportunities to teach conflict resolution because conflict is an integral part of daily life.

Take sibling fighting, for instance. What parent hasn't had questions and concerns about how to stop the kids from fighting? Worried and frustrated parents often ask me, "How can I get my kids to stop fighting and to solve problems in a peaceful way?"

It's a useful question because it concerns so many parents, yet there is no magical answer to it. However, the principles of conflict resolution that have been discussed in this chapter apply to brothers and sisters fighting and having disagreements as much as they apply to any other conflict in life. As I have stressed throughout this book, though, if you view sibling fighting as another stressor and then treat the problem as a misbehavior or as a situation requiring punishment, then you are likely to miss out on a golden opportunity.

My two children were fairly normal kids when it came to squabbles and disagreements. Jill, almost five years older than Jason, tended to resent his intrusion into her life. When they were younger (they're both now adults in their twenties), she often treated him like a second-class citizen and sometimes more like a slave to be pushed around and bullied than a brother to be respected. This made it difficult for the two of them to come to agreement on various issues, such as where to eat lunch or what movie to see or where to go on vacation.

When they were still young, my wife and I wanted them not only to get along but to learn to solve problems without the kind of serious disagreement that often erupted into verbal or physical interaction. When they had one of their arguments, I refused to take sides and told them they had to reach an agreement between themselves. I would stipulate that it had to be settled by talking and both of them would have to agree on the solution.

Sometimes this approach had the immediate effect of presenting Jill with an opportunity to berate Jason for not being more agreeable—which meant seeing her point of view and doing it her way. If she took this approach, he dug in his heels and would refuse to agree to anything she suggested. When I could see that this wasn't getting them anywhere, I would point this out and suggest that they each needed to come up with ways to solve the problem, forgetting for the moment that the other might not like their ideas.

As they got older, they were able to do some brainstorming. As they brainstormed ideas, they had to eventually settle on one idea. That meant a compromise had to take place. In the end, they would come to an agreement (even though my wife and I tended to sometimes hasten their collective willingness to compromise by suggesting that we would make the decision if they didn't and neither one would like what we chose). Usually the idea would be announced by one of them, and it would go like this:

"Dad, we agreed that we'll go to the movie Jill wants to see today and I get to pick the movie next week. Is that okay?"

I would respond with something like this: "Jason, are you in agreement with this? We'll go to Jill's pick today and yours next week? Everyone likes this idea?"

When each said yes in a tone that really did indicate agreement, that was the deal. If either Jill or Jason was half-hearted about it, I asked more questions or sent them back to bargaining. But if both agreed, then it was settled.

FIVE-STEP METHOD FOR CONFLICT RESOLUTION

You can use an even more formal method by actually teaching children a set of steps and requiring that they not only learn them but follow them when trying to work out a problem.

I know this may be tough to believe, but the teens I work with are able to learn and use a more formal method of conflict resolution. They have to understand the steps in the process and to practice by role-playing several times before they can use it in real-life situations. Many elementary schools around the country teach children a series of steps similar to the ones I will describe here, and I have seen students using this kind of conflict resolution procedure in the hallway and on the playground.

Here are the five steps you can teach teens that would be useful in resolving many different kinds of problems or disagreements:

1. What's Our Problem?

The problem has to be defined and stated. For instance, a young teenaged boy might say, "I want to get my ear pierced, and you're against it." The parent would have to agree that that indeed was what the conflict was about.

2. How Can We Solve It?

Both people in the dispute would have to begin brainstorming the problem to generate several possible ways of solving it. In the example of the boy wanting his ear pierced, one idea could be that he would wear a simple, small earring that wouldn't be gaudy or offensive and that he would take it out for formal occasions. Another could be that he would wait until he was 16 years old. Or they could ask someone they both respected if it would be okay if a boy his age wore an earring.

3. What's the Best Solution?

After generating several possible solutions, both parties have to evaluate the ideas. That means looking at the consequence of each idea and trying to figure out what would happen if that idea was selected. Using the example laid out in step two, if the parent and the teenager tried to determine the outcome if he used a small, but high-quality earring, the parent could say, "Yes, but that might be to placate me at first and later you would switch to an earring I didn't like." Or the teen might say, "If

I wait until I'm sixteen, you might push it to a later date when my birthday came."

4. Pick One and Try It

By evaluating each solution in this way, the two sides could then decide which was the best idea for him. Having picked one, the next step is to use it.

5. How Did It Work Out?

After trying it, both the adolescent and his parent would each have to ask themselves, "How did I do? Did this turn out the way I thought it would?"

If it had a successful outcome, both could give themselves a pat on the back or feel good about their efforts. If, on the other hand, it wasn't such a successful result, they might decide to try a different type of solution in the future.

As I said earlier, it's been my experience that when children and teens learn these steps and rehearse them several times, they will use the method.

I remember the first time I became convinced of this. I had been teaching a group of six teenagers who had serious behavior problems about the steps, and we practiced and role-played it in group therapy sessions. One day soon after this, I arrived late to our session. As I walked in, one of the boys asked for the pad of paper he knew I always carried with me.

When I handed it to him, along with my pen, he said, "Okay, Richard, now what's the problem? You say your mother won't let you use the car on Saturday night to go to the concert with your girlfriend. Right?"

As I watched, he went through each step of the conflict resolution method, writing down the question and Richard's responses. All of the other teenagers in the group were huddled around offering their suggestions. I stayed out of it, and Richard, along with assistance from others in this therapy group, rejected his own initial idea to "borrow" his mother's car without permission. Together they came up with a workable solution: Richard would ask his mother if he could go with a friend who was able to drive.

I could hardly wait for the next group session a week later.

"How did your problem work out?" I asked Richard.

"Great," he replied. "My ma said yes, and me and my girlfriend went with this other guy and everything was cool. I didn't get in any trouble or anything."

"Cool," I responded.

PUTTING IT INTO ACTION

Choose one or more of the following three activities to teach your teen healthy conflict resolution.

1. Have your teen practice using the Seven Quick Resolution Tools for Minor Conflicts by showing that she can apply them in the following situations:

- Her friend wants her to go to a movie, but your teen would rather stay home and watch TV. (Flip a coin)

- Her boyfriend and she are arguing about her talking to another boy. It's starting to get very emotional and heated. (Walk away or Skip it)

- A girl at school teases her about a jacket she's wearing. (Laugh it off or Walk away)

- She comes home later than her curfew and you are angry with her. (Say you're sorry or Be agreeable)

- A teacher criticizes her in front of the whole class. (Laugh it off, Skip it, or Be agreeable)

- A girl in the hallway at school intentionally bumps into her and then calls her an uncomplimentary name. (Laugh it off, Skip it, or Walk away)

- A teacher lost her homework and asks her to do it over. (Split the difference or Be agreeable)

2. Use the following situations as conflicts to role-play in order to practice finding a Win-Win Solution:

- He wants to work after school, but you think he should spend extra time on school work in order to get better grades.

- He thinks he deserves a B in algebra, but his algebra teacher says he is one percentage point low. He wants his teacher to give him that extra percentage point, but the teacher says she can't.

- He's planning to go to a rock concert with his friends on Saturday night, but you remind him that he will have to be home by his curfew, which is 11:30 P.M. He says that the concert won't even be over by then.

- Although he's been smoking for more than a year, you have just found out he's been smoking in his bedroom. You don't want him to do that and threaten to stop him from smoking in the house or on the property.

- He wants a pass to leave class in order to talk to his counselor. It's really important for him to talk to his counselor, but his teacher says to wait until after class.

- His girlfriend says she would like to go out every Friday night with her friends. He doesn't like this idea and discourages her. She insists she needs more time with her friends.

- You tell him he must clean the garage this afternoon. He's already made plans to go to the mall with several friends.

3.   Have your teen role-play and practice using the Five-Step Method for Conflict Resolution in the following situations:

- Your teen and a friend are in a store. Her friend says, "Let's take this new CD. They don't have a security system here." Your child doesn't want to steal.

- Your teen is talking to the teacher after class. The teacher says in an accusing fashion: "You were cheating on the test today and I'm going to give you a zero on it."

- Your teen is walking in the hall at school and another kid comes up to her and says, "You said something about my girl I don't like."

- Your teen has been called by a boy she doesn't like who says, "So, are you going to go with me to the party on Saturday night?"

- Your teen and his friend are working at home on some homework. His friend says to him: "Let's forget this homework. We've been at it for an hour. Let's get out of here and go to Jamie's house. Okay?"

- Your teen is being confronted by you. You say to him: "Where are you going? Do you think I'm letting you go out tonight after the way you've been acting?"

- Your teen thinks to himself: "I'd like to get high tonight because I've had lots of pressure lately. But if I do, then I won't study and I've got a test tomorrow. I'm not sure what to do."

- Your teen is talking to you and you say: "My necklace is missing and I'm sure one of your friends took it."

PART THREE

PARENTING THE DIFFICULT TEEN

8

STRATEGIES FOR PARENTING THE DIFFICULT TEEN

You've read in this book that I've worked for several years with adolescents on probation in a juvenile court. This means that the teens I see and work with every day are unusually difficult kids. All have been in trouble with the police, and many are fighters who have great difficulty getting along with other people. Most are oppositional defiant teens who go against the rules and consistently defy the wishes of adults. Some are worse and are diagnosed as having conduct disorder. A teen with conduct disorder has serious behavior problems and often has little regard for rules, laws, or the needs or the feelings of others.

Your teen may be somewhat oppositional and break rules, or she or he may even be as tough as the ones with whom I work. This chapter is intended to assure you that there is always hope and that there are ways that you can approach your teen and teach him or her that offer you opportunities to help your teen make changes. Based on my work with very difficult teenagers, I have a strong belief that with only a few exceptions most tough kids can learn the social skills they need to be more successful in life.

Chapters 2 through 7 gave you some of the strategies you can use to help improve your teen's social skills. This chapter will more specifically tell you how to handle a particularly difficult teen while you're trying to teach those skills.

Psychologists and therapists like Eva Feindler and Arnold Goldstein have given us excellent tools for helping tough adolescents learn to manage anger and to resolve conflicts peacefully. But as you take on the job of teaching these same skills to your child, you'll encounter similar problems to the ones those of us on the battlefront in juvenile courts and adolescent treatment centers face day in and day out.

Questions you may ask yourself while raising your difficult adolescent could be some of the following:

- How do I best confront him?
- How should I deal with her anger toward me?
- How can I control him without being controlling and mean?
- How should I handle her oppositional behavior?
- How can I deal with his low motivation to learn?
- How can I best handle my teen when she's involved in serious misbehavior?

In the next several pages, I will answer these questions.

HOW DO I BEST CONFRONT MY TEENAGER?

Confrontation with a difficult teenager is inevitable. Either his behavior makes a confrontation necessary, or he sets up the confrontation in order to show you that you're an inadequate or unnecessarily angry parent. But what's the best way of handling the confrontation?

Whether the confrontation is initiated by you or by the teen, there's one very important thing to keep in mind: Every interaction with an adolescent is a golden opportunity to model and to teach respect, control, and the appropriate handling of problems. What this really means, of course, is that as a teacher of your child, you should have exemplary social skills. It would be wonderful if it were so. But none of us is perfect when it comes to using social skills. We all have our flaws.

Despite the fact that I teach social skills, I certainly don't always say or do the right thing. On the other hand, I've had hundreds of opportunities to practice using social skills with difficult teenagers. But if you feel that you're not equipped to deal with your teen, there are a couple of things I can recommend: The first is to take this book seriously for yourself and reread Chapters 2 through 7 with the idea that you're going to learn all of the social skills yourself. The second is to find opportunities to practice your own social skills. You can do this by using the action plan at the end of each chapter and writing out answers and responses. Or find a friend, partner, or spouse and practice role-playing, especially in those areas where you feel you have your greatest weaknesses.

In order to confront a difficult teenager successfully, you need to have fairly adept social skills in the areas of anger control and conflict resolution. So, reread Chapters 6 and 7 and become as skilled as you can so that confrontations with your teenager don't fall apart because you get too angry or forget some of the essentials of conflict resolution.

Adapting to confrontations some of what I've written in previous chapters, here are some points you will need to keep in mind if you want your confrontations to work out well for both of you:

- Confront in a respectful way.
- Confront privately and without embarrassing your teen.
- Be calm.
- Don't attack or accuse.

- Listen to your teen's side of things.
- If your teen is too defensive, back off and try later.

Let's look at each of these points one by one.

Confront in a Respectful Way

No matter what the teen is doing or saying, remain polite and respectful. If you give a teen a model of disrespect and rudeness, you're obviously teaching the wrong thing.

I can remember one time when a teenage girl verbally attacked me in a group session. She was angry at what I was going to report to the juvenile court about her and what I was recommending for her future. She lost control very quickly and began screaming and swearing at me.

I had two concerns (aside from whether she would attack me physically and whether she was carrying a weapon). They were: how I could calm her down and help her get control and how I could make this a meaningful experience for her and the rest of the teens who were witnessing this confrontation.

To answer both of those questions, I had to remain polite and respectful to her. If I attacked her back, if I said anything that was demeaning, or if I was at all disrespectful to her as a person, both she and the other teenagers present would see me less as a role model and more as a villain.

I allowed her to vent her rage and her anger, but I also began to acknowledge her feelings. "I know you're very angry at me right now," I said. "I know you don't like what I'm recommending for you."

At first she couldn't even hear what I was saying. So I repeated my acknowledgments of her feelings, but added her name: "Terrie, I know you're angry at me right now, and I don't blame you. If I were in your situation, I would be angry, too."

Then, I wanted to get her to think and to operate less on pure emotion. To do that I asked a question. "Terrie, what part of my recommendation for you do you think is unfair?" If she was to answer this, she would have to use her brain.

"That I should stay on probation to the court for six more months," Terrie replied.

"And you don't think that was fair of me to recommend, right?" I asked.

"That's right!" she shouted.

"You may be right," I said. "Perhaps it wasn't fair."

That slowed her down even more. I was agreeing with her. But then I wanted to get her to remember who I was and what I really felt about her. "Terrie, you've known me for a long time," I said. "In all the time you've known me, have I ever done anything that showed you I was against you or wanted things to turn out badly for you?"

She had to stop and think about that. After a few seconds, she shook her head and said, "No."

At this point, I knew Terrie's anger was dissipated and that she could calm herself. We carried on a more rational discussion after that. I could explain the reasons for my recommendation, and she could voice her anger, hurt, and fear.

Anytime you're in an angry confrontation with a teen, you do not want to give them an excuse to escalate their behavior into physical violence. If you allow yourself to be either disrespectful or impolite, you give them that ready excuse.

Confront Privately and without Embarrassing Your Teen

If you're initiating the confrontation, choose a private time and place. Most confrontations don't have to occur immediately. Many are based on several instances of behavior after which you decide that a confrontation is necessary to deal with the situation that is developing.

So, it's best to get your child alone where she will likely be less defensive and will not feel a need to pose in front of peers. Most teens, if confronted in front of others, will have to play whatever role they've developed. If that role is one of a tough kid, then they will be forced to play that out in a group. You won't be able to crack their tough-guy facade, and your public confrontation may force them to take it farther in order to prove how tough they are to the others who are watching.

The second thing that takes place in a group or a social setting is that kids may feel embarrassed or humiliated. While some parents (or other adults) may feel like there is some value in humiliating a teen, I don't see this. Difficult teens frequently have some self-esteem problems hidden underneath their tough exterior, and embarrassing them in front of others is setting up an entirely unpredictable situation. You don't know how your adolescent will handle this. It could easily blow up in your face with unexpected explosive behavior.

In addition, there is the strong possibility that you will lose whatever respect he has for you.

Be Calm

Don't lose your cool, especially if you're being confronted by the teen. Stay calm and use the conflict resolution skills I've outlined in Chapter 7.

This requires that you have your own anger under control. Try not to get angry, or if you do, don't let it show so much that you lose control of your emotions and risk escalating the situation.

Use the anger-management skills outlined in Chapter 6. Taking deep breaths, taking a break and turning on some soothing music, visualizing a quiet, restful place, or using progressive relaxation can help you return to a calm state.

Other ways to stay calm are consciously lowering your voice, making sure the television is turned off before you begin talking, and using active listening. Lowering your voice helps you to stay more relaxed and in control. Active listening techniques can move you from a passive recipient of the anger being directed at you to an active listener less concerned with your own pride or ego and more concerned with helping your teenager calm himself.

Active listening methods that can serve you well in a confrontation are:

- Mirroring feelings.

- Reflecting meanings.

- Clarifying possible solutions with questions.

Mirroring feelings helps you to listen carefully, takes your mind off the injustice of the other person's attack, and allows you to focus on what's really important. What is important is assisting your teen to get his feelings under control. By mirroring what he feels, you help him to put his emotions into words while he begins to get a sense that you understand what he's experiencing.

For instance, if your teenager is attacking you for being so unfeeling and unsympathetic, your mirroring statement would be: "It sounds like you feel like I don't care about you" or "You feel angry that I don't show you any sympathy."

This kind of active listening response on your part almost always leads the teen either to agree or to disagree. To do either, she has to think about what you've said. And that, of course, is what you want an upset, confrontive teen to do: think, rather than just emote.

Reflecting meanings is vital because you want to establish some common ground between you. You want to establish that you understand your teen's upset and concern and that the two of you have some ability to connect on the problem.

Just as with mirroring feelings, reflecting meanings is a way of summarizing what has been said and what both of you mean. You could say, "So you feel angry because I never listen to you and you hate me so much that you wish I was out of your life. Right?" or "You feel like running away because I wasn't around for you when you were younger and now you don't care if we have a relationship?"

Clarifying possible solutions with questions allows you to get a clear understanding of your teen's feelings and an indication that you know what he means. For instance, you could ask, "Have you felt like I wasn't there for you for a long time?" or "Was there something I did recently that made you so angry?"

The most important questions have to do with what you can do about the situation to make it better. By asking, "How can we work on this problem so you don't have to leave home?" you can move the discussion to a productive level.

Sometimes, however, adolescents are so upset, so angry, or by temperament so pessimistic that they are not able to think of a solution right then. That's all right. Conflicts don't have to be resolved in a specified period of time. Maybe your teen needs time to cool off and to think about the situation. Maybe you both need time to reflect on ways to solve the problem. You can talk about it later.

Don't Attack or Accuse

Although I've made this point several times, it's important enough that I want to emphasize it again: You're not going to handle a confrontation successfully by attacking or by accusing your teenager.

That only deflects the thrust of the teen's attack from you back to her. That's a defensive reaction, but also a very human one. However, we're talking about dealing with a tough teen, and you have to deal with a tough teen differently from the way you might deal with a child who is easier to get along with.

If you are guilty of whatever your teen may be accusing you of, the best defense is to admit it. Once you've admitted it and taken away some of her upset or anger, you still have to decide how to prevent this from happening again. If you are not guilty, then wait for her anger to cool before trying to explain your side of things.

Listen to Your Teen's Side of Things

Your child has his own side of things, and his own point of view. You don't have to defend yourself or answer the charges against you. And certainly don't do this by interrupting what he's saying. Instead, listen respectfully and take what your child is saying seriously.

Don't neglect this and don't undermine his interest in telling you about it. Give him a chance to explain his side of things. Then you can use active listening methods to deal with what he's saying. A difficult adolescent will be easier to deal with if he feels that you understand him.

If He's Too Defensive, Back Off and Try Later

Sometimes, no matter how well you use the skills I've outlined in this book, the teen will be too angry or too defensive to begin to sort out possible solutions to the problem.

If that is so, then it's often better to back off and decide how you might tackle the problem again at a later time. You may also, by delaying action, find a better approach to dealing with the confrontation.

CONFRONTING IN THE RIGHT WAY

It's important to decide what you're going to say to your teen if you're doing the confronting. What do you need to confront about? Teens sometimes need to be confronted about behaviors they're not doing anything about, that is, problem behaviors that might have been going on for some time. You've given them opportunities to handle it on their own, but nothing is changing. A talk is in order.

Let's take an example of a teenager who is not handling school well. Suppose Darius has been given a chance to bring his high school grades up, but his latest report card just arrived and it shows that his social studies grade has slipped to a D and history is an I (incomplete). You believe you can't let this go on without saying something. But how do you confront in an appropriate way?

The words you start with are important. You can simply bring up the subject ("I think we need to talk about your grades"), or you can make an appointment for a later time ("Can we talk about something important after dinner?").

What can happen even if you start the confrontation in this benign way? Well certainly things can go wrong. Your teen may try to avoid it. She may know what's coming next and may think you're going to yell at her. Or she may feel guilty and may want to wiggle out of the confrontation. Or she just may not want to have to change.

Sometimes in their defensiveness, teens get very angry immediately. Then, you have to calm them down, defuse their anger, or relieve the tension before you can even begin to deal with the issue at hand.

If your teen gets too angry too quickly, you have to take some fairly quick action. Everything I've written in this chapter applies, but there are proven methods to defuse anger that should be reemphasized.

One good method is to acknowledge his feelings. "I know you're angry about me bringing this up," is one way to show that you know how he feels. Let him know quickly that you know exactly how he feels. You can even sympathize with those feelings by saying, "I know you're angry and I probably would be too if I thought someone was going to yell at me because of my grades."

Sometimes an expression of regret can help defuse some of the anger. You could say, "I'm sorry I have to talk to you about your grades when I know you'd prefer not to deal with the situation. But I think your grades are too important to just let go."

At times asking her how she feels about talking about it can assist in dealing with the underlying feelings. "You seem angry about my questioning you about your grades. Are you? I'm just wondering how you feel about my bringing the subject up."

As a final comment regarding kids who get mad easily during a confrontation, I think it's important that you never use physical means or your own escalating anger to try to gain control over the teen or to force them to get control. Slapping them, pushing them around, grabbing them forcefully, getting in their face, yelling, and similar methods are almost always doomed to failure.

I've dealt with kids after adults have used these methods. While they might change their behavior for the moment, the lingering resentment and hostility engendered by such methods have a long-lasting negative effect that far outweighs any potential benefits.

DEALING WITH YOUR CHILD'S ANGER TOWARD YOU

If the anger is only occasional, it's easier to take. If it's frequent or constant, it's more distressing and keeps tensions much too high.

For example, when Erin told her mother angrily that she was so mad at her that she didn't want to have a mother-daughter relationship anymore, her mother was confused and saddened. "I've tried so hard to be a good mother all her life," Erin's mother said. "Now she doesn't even want me to be her mother. How am I supposed to act? I am her mother."

Anger has to be talked about, and that means a confrontation at some point. Often teens don't want to quit on the relationship with you, but they may be disappointed about it or feel it's useless to try to fix it. By getting your teen to talk about her anger, perhaps you can perk up her willingness to continue to invest in the relationship.

CONTROLLING WITHOUT BEING CONTROLLING

Many parents believe they must be in control of their adolescent child. But is it a good thing for parents to be in total control of their teen?

The answer is a qualified yes. Let me explain. While control of infants and toddlers is important because they need us to protect them, as kids grow older the amount of control we have to exert in the interest of protection diminishes. Our job is not so much one of having control and mastery over a teen as it is being a teacher, a trainer, and a consultant.

I often compare the situation of parenting a teenager to that of training a tiger in the circus. When a tiger outweighs and can outmaneuver a trainer, the tiger doesn't give up his strength and power except as he's willing to do so. He can hurt the trainer any time he chooses to. A teenager doesn't *have* to listen to or obey a parent. He does so only because he agrees that this is what he wishes to do. He realizes that the parent provides some essentials in life—

like food, shelter, love, and the car. In addition, he should regard his parent as a wise teacher, a trainer who can keep him safe, and a consultant to whom he can go when there are problems.

But what if you don't quite have that relationship with your teen? What if you have tried to maintain complete power and control? What if he now resents your efforts to have control over him and won't consent to be governed?

Then you have a real challenge, but not an insurmountable one. I've seen parents make significant changes in their relationship with their teens. By explaining that they are giving up their previous control, they have been able to come to a reasonable agreement with their teenagers about rules. Don't give up on your child, but consider giving up your need to dominate or to control him. I think this is one of those situations where a friendly confrontation is called for. The purpose is to put the situation and the relationship in perspective and to try to reach an agreement.

You might say something like this: "You know, Brad, we've had a lot of arguments lately, and I know you resent my efforts to impose controls on you. You don't like my rules and you get angry with me. I have been doing a lot of thinking about us, and I think I've made some mistakes. For instance, I've tried to control you like you were a little kid, and I don't blame you for being mad about this. I think we have to come up with a new way of handling things if we're going to get along until you're old enough to move out on your own. What I'd like to propose is that we talk about our relationship and what we need from each other. Okay?"

With this kind of beginning, you have a chance to move in a couple of different directions. If Brad wishes to even have this talk, you can begin talking about the relationship and what he would like for that relationship. In one recent conversation like this between a parent and a 16-year-old, the teen said that she wanted a friendship with her mother with both of them on an equal basis in the relationship. That was very hard for the mother to swallow. And it would perhaps be impossible. Yet, it was a starting point for a discussion.

The alternative to this mother automatically rejecting this idea was that her 16-year-old daughter was threatening to move out the day she turned 17.

The other direction such a discussion can take is about ground rules for living together. It's very difficult for parents to just arbitrarily impose rules on a teenager who refuses to obey them. It's often much better to agree on certain rules they would *both* live by in order for life to go more smoothly for everyone. In such discussions, limits and house rules must be discussed. Teens may express a wish to live without rules, but most also agree that most limits make sense when they're discussed in the context of a family.

In being a parent after giving up control, you have to redefine for yourself what your role is. I think the parent of every adolescent has to do this at some time or another. When a teen is spending more time at school and work and sports than at home, when a teen is away at college, or when a teen is working full-time, the way you use your authority and the terms of the relationship change. For both parent and child this can be a difficult adjustment.

DEALING WITH OPPOSITIONAL BEHAVIOR

It is inevitable, particularly if you have a difficult teen, that you're going to have to deal with oppositional behavior. Most parents have faced oppositional behavior at one time or another since their child was a toddler.

But there's a difference between a 38-pound toddler telling you No and a 6-foot-tall, 176-pound teenage boy telling you No. This doesn't feel like you're dealing with a child, and you suddenly realize that there isn't one thing you can do to change the situation.

But there are things you can do to deal with the situation. They might not sound very satisfying or effective, yet I spend most of my professional life with oppositional and rebellious adolescents, most of whom are bigger and stronger than I am, and I survive. And my groups don't get out of control—at least not very often.

What's the trick? Very simple: *Avoid power struggles*. You can't win power struggles unless you have complete control over a teen, and most of us don't have complete power and control. Even if we did, it's not very satisfying to have kids do things our way just because we have more absolute power than they do.

Refusing to engage in power struggles is important. In effect, when you do this, you are acknowledging that it is true they don't have to do anything if they choose not to.

I usually say this to teens: "You're right. I can't make you do that" or "I can't force you to do what I'm asking. But," I add, "I'd like for you to do it."

Now, does this work? Often, but not always. But the way I phrase my statements is realistic and lets her know she has a choice. I can't force her to do anything, and I'm not trying to exert force and control. I'm asking. For many oppositional, tough teens, that feels different. They tell me they're tired of adults pushing them around telling them what they have to do and trying to force them to do whatever it is they want them to do.

Sometimes it helps to use a little trick. That trick is to use their oppositional tendencies against them. We know they are oppositional and go against things. Telling them, "Do this" is a red flag to an oppositional teen. You know they will react by saying, "Make me" or "No way." To use their oppositional tendencies, tell them to do something that will allow them to rebel, but by so doing they actually do what you want.

Sound a little confusing? Here's an example that may help. You could say, "I know this will be very hard for you to do and you probably won't be able to do it." In this case, if they're going to be oppositional, the only true way in which they can be so is by proving they can do what you've said they'd have trouble doing.

Along the same lines, you could say, "I know you won't want to do this and you'll probably refuse to do it, but I'm asking you to do it anyway." Again, if he is going to be really oppositional he'll do it. This is not a technique to be used with just any teen. It should be reserved for special occasions with oppositional and defiant teens, and used only once in a while.

You can also phrase a direction in terms of a request. So, if you say, "Would you do me a favor by completing this work?" then they understand that they can decide not to do it and that they're not being forced to do it. It is up to them.

DEALING WITH LOW MOTIVATION

In teaching social skills to oppositional teens, you'll frequently find that they have low motivation to do something different or to learn a skill. It helps if you show them how a new skill will benefit them. It also helps if you wait for a golden opportunity that allows you to demonstrate a skill that helps them deal with an aspect of their life.

Finally, we all have low motivation when the work is presented in boring, nonchallenging ways. The following are some of the techniques I've found that are dramatic, challenging, and fun and that tend to work well with difficult teenagers:

- Set up a competition.
- Give attractive prizes for successful completion of a task.
- Make a fun game out of learning.
- Give teens a role to play in the teaching.
- Make a videotape of them practicing their new skills.
- Use your own personal experiences to teach lessons.

HANDLING A TEEN WHO IS INVOLVED
IN SERIOUS MISBEHAVIOR

Your teenager may be one of the few who present more serious behavior problems. Whereas many teenagers will be oppositional or defiant or even get arrested for some delinquent act, only a small percentage (most studies suggest that it's less than 10 percent) are actually guilty of regular criminal behavior, the selling of drugs, gang activities, or incorrigible behavior at home or school.

Such teens are frequently labelled as having an oppositional defiant disorder or having a conduct disorder. But these psychiatric labels serve little purpose for parents—except to scare them or to make the problem appear insurmountable.

It's not helpful to view your adolescent as a delinquent or a criminal. It is, on the other hand, helpful to see him simply as a teenager who sometimes presents serious behavior problems. That in fact is more accurate. Even the most delinquent teen will at times be kind, goal-oriented, productive, and even lovable. But the difference in outlook for you is enormous. Think of your teen as having a conduct disorder, and you're more likely to see him as unable to change. But think of him as a teenager with problem behavior, and you can envision reducing that undesirable behavior.

So, even if your teen has been arrested, charged with a crime, or placed in a detention facility, it's not necessarily the end of the world. The facts are surprisingly optimistic. Membership in teenage gangs, for instance, is transitory, and few adults remain in gangs. Most teens who get arrested, placed on probation, or sent to a delinquent treatment center do not go on to a life of crime. The majority of adolescents who run away from home, assault their parents, or have serious communication problems with their parents aren't permanently isolated from their families.

Many work out a better and closer relationship as they become young adults. Most of the teenagers with whom I work in my groups make positive changes in their lives and get dismissed from probation. I've had the good fortune of being able to keep in touch with some teens whom I met in the juvenile court. Usually when I hear from them ten or twenty years later, they are leading useful, productive lives as good citizens.

But for you to turn your teen around and help her get on the right path won't just happen as if by magic. Giving up on your teen or refusing to have anything to do with her will certainly not make things better. Taking some kind of positive action will.

As I've already suggested throughout this book, you can look for golden opportunities to teach social skills, and you can work on your relationship as well as your communication with your teen. But there's more that you have to do if your teenager is involved in serious delinquent or antisocial behavior. There are five steps you can take:

1. Strive to understand the causes of her problems.
2. View your teen's problems as part of an overall family problem.
3. Draw on the strengths of your family.
4. Use outside resources.
5. Be persistent.

UNDERSTANDING THE CAUSES OF TEENAGE PROBLEMS

It would be easy to bury your head in the sand and hope the problem goes away on its own. It's also relatively easy to disown your child and say, "It's his problem." It's also easy to blame his bad friends, drugs, inadequate teachers, and the media.

Although it's a lot harder to do a serious review of your family life, the social history of your child, and the various influences on him to try to get a clearer picture of what went wrong, it's also more likely to be beneficial.

With the problems that your teen presents in sharper focus, you can take a more objective view of him and the reason for his problems. That will lead to an understanding of your role in your teen's difficulties.

VIEWING YOUR TEEN'S PROBLEMS AS PART OF AN OVERALL FAMILY PROBLEM

Don't just point the finger at your teen and conclude that you did everything right as a parent. By taking the first step and looking for influences and causes of your teen's problems, you should be able to see some ways you contributed to her behavior. As parents, we play an important role in our kids' behaviors.

For example, teenagers rarely gravitate toward a gang unless there are serious problems at home. For a teen to be attracted to a gang means that she has a need for some aspects of family life missing at home—companionship, affection, friendship, and protection.

Another example is teens who run away from home. Surveys of runaway youth show that more than half of them leave home because they have serious communication problems with their parents. Most kids who run away have explored other alternatives first and only as a last resort do they run in order to escape a home life that has become too painful.

By putting your teen's problems in the context of the family, it makes getting help that much easier. Teens often resent being fingered as the troublemaker in the family. They are much more receptive to getting help when the rest of the family is involved.

Family therapy has been found in numerous studies to be an effective approach to dealing with a teen with serious behavior problems.

DRAWING ON THE STRENGTHS OF YOUR FAMILY

Your family, like most families, has both weaknesses and strengths. The strengths of your family can be useful in dealing with your difficult teenager.

When you have a teenager who is involved in serious behavior problems, you can allow this situation to tear your family apart or you can draw on the strengths and resources of the family to better deal with the problem.

When 16-year-old Audrey was arrested for shoplifting, was fighting regularly with her parents, and had already run away once, the whole family held a meeting. Audrey's parents invited both sets of grandparents, an aunt and an uncle, and Audrey's siblings to the meeting. Discussing together how they could all help out, one set of grandparents volunteered to have Audrey live with them temporarily. Audrey agreed and within days had moved in with her grandparents.

The few weeks she lived with her grandparents allowed time for the rift with her parents to heal and for more effective communication to take effect. Both Audrey and her parents had a respite from the everyday emotional crises that were so draining. But by drawing on the closeness and the helpfulness of the extended family, this family was able to better deal with Audrey's problems.

Other families have strengths that are unique. Some families have communication skills. Others are able to offer emotional support to one another. Still others have a sense of humor, membership in a religious community, or the ability to persevere in a crisis without letting problems cause permanent damage to the family.

USING OUTSIDE RESOURCES

Often families in which there is a troubled teen feel isolated and different from other families. If you remain isolated, it will be more difficult to deal with your own feelings, which often include shame and guilt. But by reaching out to your community and taking advantage of the resources available to you, you can combat the feeling of isolation while getting some needed help. What can the community offer you?

First there are therapists, including family therapists, who specialize in helping families with a tough teenager. By asking friends, neighbors, or your doctor for recommendations, you can usually locate these specialists.

Second, there are support groups and parent training groups that can help you to feel less alone and to find other people with problems similar to yours. Toughlove, an organization that has been around for many years, is designed specifically to offer parents of very-hard-to-manage teenagers the support and help of other parents. Attending parent training classes can increase your skills so that you are better prepared to deal appropriately with your teen.

Also, there are hospitals and treatment centers that provide both inpatient and outpatient services for adolescents and their families when the problems become overwhelming. Frequently medical insurance will assist in paying for such services. A teen's short stay in a psychiatric hospital designed for kids with problems can help prepare both the adolescent and the family for treatment following this cooling off period. Another benefit of a short hospitalization is that sometimes teens can be stabilized on medication that can assist in smoothing out some of the troubled behavior.

Finally, there are juvenile and family courts. Although many families wish to avoid the stigma of having a child in the judicial system, sometimes this is the best alternative. Juvenile courts have a tradition of trying to help young people rather than just trying to punish them. Many of these courts have diversion programs, psychological clinics, and a variety of social services that can truly help some children.

In addition, of course, juvenile and family courts have the full power of the legal system. This adds weight to what is recommended by the court, and this can be a welcome relief to parents who find they have lost their influence or their ability to enforce rules and guidelines at home. Occasionally, some teenagers need to be removed from home for the protection of their family or the community. This may be troubling to you, but for many teens I know this is a wake-up call that helps them to realize that they must learn to live within the laws and the limits imposed by their family or the community.

BEING PERSISTENT

I hope one of my messages is clear throughout this book: Difficult behavior by your teen is not a reason to give up on her or him. Furthermore, difficult teen behavior requires your strength to try to help your teen learn new skills and new patterns of behavior. To do this, though, you must be strong and must summon up the courage to hang in there with your tough teen.

In short, you must persevere. Take heart from what I've written about the fact that most difficult teenagers will be able to make changes if they receive help. The help they need the most, though, is your love, your willingness to stick with them when times are tough, and your ability to persist even when they act like they don't want your help and don't care if you believe in them. Most of that is a facade. It is not what they want or necessarily what they feel.

Difficult and tough teens are still teenagers. No matter how tough they are on the outside, on the inside they are still often insecure, frightened kids who want help in negotiating this rough world in which they live.

They need the skills we can teach them. They just don't always know it. They frequently think they know everything already because they've lived for fifteen or sixteen years in a public school or a violent neighborhood. They've had a lot of experiences that they sometimes think qualify them to be adults. The fact is, though, that they don't have what we can offer—skills and experience.

They need us. We just have to let them know how and when they need us. And when they do need us, we have to be there for them.

AFTERWORD

Raising a teenager is a perilous task even under the best of circumstances. There are always bumps and detours along the way toward adulthood. Teenagers rebel against authority, resent being told what to do, want to fight against injustice, take up the habits of peers, dress weirdly, listen to music that couldn't even be recorded when you were their age, and use words that would have gotten your generation arrested.

If you're able to step back for a moment and put your teenager in perspective, you'll probably find that he or she is a pretty good kid who most of the time has great social skills. But you don't live in this detached, objective way. You live in a family with day-to-day interactions and where you get to see both the best and, unfortunately, the worst of your teen. You see your child's warts, foibles, peculiarities, and hang-ups.

A socially skilled teen? You wonder. Maybe you missed the boat. After reading this book, you think you missed out somewhere.

SKILLS FOR PARENTS

It's never easy to be the parent of a teenager, but there are some skills *you* need in order to best survive your kid's teenage years.

Developing the skills of showing respect and taking your teen's needs into consideration are important. So is the skill of keeping your own hostile and angry feelings under control. If you can remember to recognize not only your teen's weaknesses but his strengths, you will be a step closer to surviving the teenage years. Also, being able to listen to her gripes and complaints will improve your relationship and the quality of your communication with each other. Finally, if you can learn to teach social skills in

200

interesting and fun ways, your teen will more readily learn all the valuable things you have to teach.

If you wish your teenager to be able to withstand the slings and arrows of an increasingly outrageous and violent world, then he must be socially competent. That, of course, means in part that he has excellent social skills. These don't just happen. They must be taught. And that is your job—to teach social skills.

SKILLS FOR TEENS

To give your teen the best chance of succeeding in life, make sure that he or she:

- Is well prepared with the skills I've written about in this book.

- Is able to set goals for the present and the future.

- Has the ability to look at self-defeating behaviors and is capable of doing something about them.

- Has the ability to communicate in an assertive way to avoid being either passive or aggressive.

- Has feelings for others and is able to understand and communicate how another person might feel.

- Is skilled at resolving conflicts in peaceful ways.

- Has the ability to keep anger under control in all relationships.

These are the things that make teens competent and skilled and that give them the tools they need to be successful in life. And once teens are taught these skills, they make you the parent of an emotionally intelligent teenager.

RESOURCES

VIDEOS

Here are some recommended videos covering the areas presented in this book. The contact information for each company is listed after the list of videos:

Anger

"Anger: You Can Handle It"—24-minute video. Sunburst Communications.
"Just Chill! Dealing with Anger"—36-minute video. Sunburst Communications.

Assertiveness

"Be Your Best Self: Assertiveness Training"—29-minute video. Sunburst Communications.

Conflict Resolution

"Strength: A Conflict Resolution Video"—12-minute video. HRM Video.
"How to Cope with School Violence"—22-minute video. The Bureau for At-Risk Youth.
"Tug of War: Strategies for Conflict Resolution"—25-minute video. HRM Video.

202

"Conflict Resolution"—26-minute video. Sunburst Communications.

Goal-Setting

"Goals"—16-minute video. ETR Associates.
"Get a Goal! Get a Life!"—27-minute video. Sunburst Communications.

Self-Defeating Behavior

"Risk-Taking and You"—23-minute video. HRM Video.
"Self-Defeating Behavior: How to Stop It"—40-minute video. HRM Video.
"Please God, I'm Only 17"—37-minute video. Churchill Media.

Companies That Produce and Distribute Social Skills Videos

Aims Multimedia
9710 DeSoto Avenue
Chatsworth, CA 91311-4409
800-367-2467

The Bureau for At-Risk Youth
645 New York Avenue
Huntington, NY 11743-4207
800-999-6884

Churchill Media
6901 Woodley Avenue
Van Nuys, CA 91406-4844
800-334-7830

Daniel Memorial Institute
6700 Southpoint Parkway
Suite 100
Jacksonville, FL 32216
800-226-7612

ETR Associates
P.O. Box 1830
Santa Cruz, CA 95061-1830
800-321-4407

HRM Video
175 Tompkins Avenue
Pleasantville, NY 10570-9973
800-431-2050

Research Press
Dept. 231
P.O. Box 9177
Champaign, IL 61826
800-519-2707

Sunburst Communications, Inc.
101 Castleton Street
P.O. Box 40
Pleasantville, NY 10570
800-431-1934

Resources for Borrowing Social Skill Videos

Occasionally your local video store will carry some videos that may have social skills themes. Such videos can often be found in the Special Interest section.

If you can't locate any of the videos listed, you can try these resources from which many social skills videos can be rented:

County Health Department—Audio-Visual Department
Local Public Library
Local College or University Library
Intermediate School District Audio-Visual Department or
   Library

BOOKS

Michael L. Bloomquist. *Skills Training for Children with Behavior Disorders: A Parent and Therapist Guidebook.* New York: Guilford Press, 1996.

Robert Bolton. *People Skills.* New York: Touchstone Books, 1986.

D. Cowan, S. Palomares, and D. Schilling. *Conflict Resolution Skills for Teens.* Spring Valley, CA: Innerchoice Publishing, 1994.

M. J. Elias and J. Clabby. *Building Social Problem Solving Skills: Guidelines from a School-Based Program.* San Francisco: Jossey-Bass, 1992.

Daniel Goleman. *Emotional Intelligence.* New York: Bantam Books, 1995.

GROUPS

The following organizations can be helpful in locating services and assistance for teenagers and their family:

Agency Information and Referral Service
800-621-3860

The American Association for Marriage and Family Therapy
1133 15th Street, NW, Suite 300
Washington, DC 20005-2710
202-452-0109

National Alliance for the Mentally Ill
200 N. Glebe Road, Suite 1015
Arlington, VA 22203-3754
703-524-7600

The National Mental Health Association
1021 Prince Street
Alexandria, VA 22314-2971
703-684-7722

Toughlove
P.O. Box 1069
Doylestown, PA 18901
215-348-7090

INDEX